CONVERSATIONS
WITH SCRIPTURE:
THE PSALMS

Other Books in the Series

Frederick W. Schmidt, *Conversations with Scripture: Revelation*

Kevin A. Wilson, *Conversations with Scripture: The Law*

William Brosend, *Conversations with Scripture: The Parables*

Cynthia Briggs Kittredge, *Conversations with Scripture: The Gospel of John*

Stephen L. Cook, *Conversations with Scripture: Second Isaiah*

Marcus J. Borg, *Conversations with Scripture: The Gospel of Mark*

Frederick W. Schmidt, *Conversations with Scripture: The Gospel of Luke*

C. K. Robertson, *Conversations with Scripture: The Acts of the Apostles*

Roy Heller, *Conversations with Scripture: The Book of Judges*

Judith Jones and Edmond Desueza, *Conversations with Scripture: The Book of Daniel*

John Y. H. Yieh, *Conversations with Scripture: The Gospel of Matthew*

CONVERSATIONS WITH SCRIPTURE:

THE PSALMS

L. WILLIAM COUNTRYMAN

Morehouse Publishing
NEW YORK · HARRISBURG · DENVER

Morehouse Publishing, 4775 Linglestown Road, Harrisburg, PA 17112

Morehouse Publishing, 445 Fifth Avenue, New York, NY 10016

Morehouse Publishing is an imprint of Church Publishing Incorporated.
www.churchpublishing.org

Cover design by Corey Kent

Typeset by Beth Oberholtzer

"PSALM 23" © 2010 by John August Swanson, Serigraph 15.25" x 24.25"; Los Angeles artist John August Swanson is noted for his finely detailed, brilliantly colored paintings and original prints. His works are found in the Smithsonian Institution's National Museum of American History, London's Tate Gallery, the Vatican Museum's Collection of Modern Religious Art, and the Bibliothèque Nationale, Paris. Website: www.JohnAugustSwanson.com

Library of Congress Cataloging-in-Publication Data

Countryman, Louis William, 1941–
  Conversations with scripture : the Psalms / L. William Countryman.
    p.   cm. — (Anglican Association of Biblical Scholars study series)
  Includes bibliographical references.
  ISBN 978-0-8192-2753-9 (pbk.) — ISBN 978-0-8192-2754-6 (ebook)
  1. Bible. O.T. Psalms—Criticism, interpretation, etc.   I. Title.
BS1430.52.C685 2013
223'.206—dc23
                                                            2012034391

Printed in the United States of America

To Betty and Wanda,
my beloved sisters,
this book is dedicated.

O God, whom saints and angels delight to worship in heaven: Be ever present with your servants who seek through art and music to perfect the praises offered by your people on earth; and grant to them even now glimpses of your beauty, and make them worthy at length to behold it unveiled for evermore; through Jesus Christ our Lord.

AMEN.

American Book of Common Prayer, 1979
Collect for Church Musicians and Artists, p. 819

CONTENTS

Introduction to the Series   ix

*Introduction—I Know "The LORD Is My Shepherd":
Why Would I Want to Study the Psalms?*   1

CHAPTER ONE
"Praise God in His Sanctuary...":
Songs for the Temple   5

CHAPTER TWO
"You That Stand in the House of the LORD":
The World of the Psalmists   27

CHAPTER THREE
"O Sing to the LORD a New Song":
Hymns of Praise and Songs of Worship   49

CHAPTER FOUR
"I Am Weary with My Crying":
Psalms of Lament, Trust, and Thanksgiving   67

CHAPTER FIVE
"The Heavens Are Telling the Glory of God":
Psalms of Wisdom   89

CHAPTER SIX
"One Generation Shall Laud Your Works to Another":
The Ongoing Influence of the Psalms   109

Study Guide by Sharon Pearson   133
A Personal Introduction   145

INTRODUCTION TO THE SERIES

To talk about a distinctively Anglican approach to Scripture is a daunting task. Within any one part of the larger church that we call the Anglican Communion there is, on historical grounds alone, an enormous variety. But as the global character of the church becomes apparent in ever-newer ways, the task of accounting for that variety, while naming the characteristics of a distinctive approach becomes increasingly difficult.

In addition, the examination of Scripture is not confined to formal studies of the kind addressed in this series of parish studies written by formally trained biblical scholars. Systematic theologian David Ford, who participated in the Lambeth Conference of 1998, rightly noted that although "most of us have studied the Bible over many years" and "are aware of various academic approaches to it," we have "also lived in it" and "inhabited it, through worship, preaching, teaching and meditation." As such, Ford observes, "The Bible in the Church is like a city we have lived in for a long time." We may not be able to account for the history of every building or the architecture on every street, but we know our way around and it is a source of life to each of us.[1]

That said, we have not done as much as we should in acquainting the inhabitants of that famed city with the architecture that lies within. So, as risky as it may seem, it is important to set out an introduction to the highlights of that city—which this series proposes to explore at length. Perhaps the best way in which to broach that task is to provide a handful of descriptors.

The first of those descriptors that leaps to mind is familiar, basic, and forever debated: *authoritative*. Years ago I was asked by a colleague who belonged to the Evangelical Free Church why someone with as much obvious interest in the Bible would be an Episcopal priest. I responded, "Because we read the whole of Scripture and not just the parts of it that suit us." Scripture has been and continues to play a singular role in the life of the Anglican Communion, but it has rarely been used in the sharply prescriptive fashion that has characterized some traditions.

Some have characterized this approach as an attempt to navigate a *via media* between overbearing control and an absence of accountability. But I think it is far more helpful to describe the tensions not as a matter of steering a course between two different and competing priorities, but as the complex dance necessary to live under a very different, but typically Anglican notion of authority itself. Authority shares the same root as the word "to author" and as such, refers first and foremost, not to the *power* to *control* with all that both of those words suggest, but to the capacity to *author creativity*, with all that both of those words suggest.[2] As such, the function of Scripture is to carve out a creative space in which the work of the Holy Spirit can yield the very kind of fruit associated with its work in the Church. The difficulty, of course, is that for that space to be creative, it is also necessary for it to have boundaries, much like the boundaries we establish for other kinds of genuinely creative freedom—the practice of scales for concert pianists, the discipline of work at the barré that frees the ballerina, or the guidance that parents provide for their children. Defined in this way, it is possible to see the boundaries around that creative space as barriers to be eliminated, or as walls that provide protection, but they are neither.

And so the struggle continues with the authority of Scripture. From time to time in the Anglican Communion, it has been and will be treated as a wall that protects us from the complexity of navigating without error the world in which we live. At other times, it will be treated as the ancient remains of a city to be cleared away in favor of a brave new world. But both approaches are rooted, not in the limitations of Scripture, but in our failure to welcome the creative space we have been given.

For that reason, at their best, Anglican approaches to Scripture are also *illuminative*. William Sloane Coffin once observed that the problem with Americans and the Bible is that we read it like a drunk uses a lamppost. We lean on it, we don't use it for illumination.[3] Leaning on Scripture—or having the lamppost taken out completely—are simply two very closely related ways of failing to acknowledge the creative space provided by Scripture. But once the creative space is recognized for what it is, then the importance of reading Scripture illuminatively becomes apparent. Application of the insight Scripture provides into who we are and what we might become is not something that can be prescribed or mapped out in detail. It is only a conversation with Scripture, marked by humility that can begin to spell out the particulars. Reading Scripture is, then, in the Anglican tradition a delicate and demanding task, that involves both the careful listening for the voice of God and courageous conversation with the world around us.

It is, for that reason, an approach that is also marked by *critical engagement* with the text itself. It is no accident that from 1860 to 1900 the three best-known names in the world of biblical scholarship were Anglican priests, the first two of whom were Bishops: B. F. Westcott, J. B. Lightfoot, and F. J. A. Hort. Together the three made contributions to both the church and the critical study of the biblical text that became a defining characteristic of Anglican life.

Of the three, Westcott's contribution, perhaps, best captures the balance. Not only did his work contribute to a critical text of the Greek New Testament that would eventually serve as the basis for the English Revised Version, but as Bishop of Durham he also convened a conference of Christians to discuss the arms race in Europe, founded the Christian Social Union, and mediated the Durham coal strike of 1892.

The English roots of the tradition are not the only, or even the defining characteristic of Anglican approaches to Scripture. The church, no less than the rest of the world, has been forever changed by the process of globalization, which has yielded a rich *diversity* that complements the traditions once identified with the church.

Scripture in Uganda, for example, has been read with an emphasis on private, allegorical, and revivalist applications. The result has been a tradition in large parts of East Africa which stresses the reading of Scripture on one's own; the direct application made to the contemporary situation without reference to the setting of the original text; and the combination of personal testimony with the power of public exhortation.

At the same time, however, globalization has brought that tradition into conversation with people from other parts of the Anglican Communion as the church in Uganda has sought to bring the biblical text to bear on its efforts to address the issues of justice, poverty, war, disease, food shortage, and education. In such a dynamic environment, the only thing that one can say with certainty is that neither the Anglican Communion, nor the churches of East Africa, will ever be the same again.

Authoritative, illuminative, critical, and varied—these are not the labels that one uses to carve out an approach to Scripture that can be predicted with any kind of certainty. Indeed, if the word *dynamic*—just used—is added to the list, perhaps all that one can predict is still more change! And, for that reason, there will be observers who (not without reason) will argue that the single common denominator in this series is that each of the authors also happens to be an Anglican. (There might even be a few who will dispute that!)

But such is the nature of life in any city, including one shaped by the Bible. We influence the shape of its life, but we are also shaped and nurtured by it. And if that city is of God's making, then to force our own design on the streets and buildings around us is to disregard the design that the chief architect has in mind.

—Frederick W. Schmidt
Series Editor

NOTES

1. David F. Ford, "The Bible, the World and the Church I," in *The Official Report of the Lambeth Conference 1998*, ed. J. Mark Dyer et al. (Harrisburg, PA: Morehouse,1999), 332.
2. For my broader understanding of authority, I am indebted to Eugene Kennedy and Sara C. Charles, *Authority: The Most Misunderstood Idea in America* (New York: Free Press, 1997).
3. William Sloane Coffin, *Credo* (Louisville, KY: Westminster John Knox Press, 2003), 156.

I Know "The LORD Is My Shepherd"

Why Would I Want to Study the Psalms?

Psalm 23 must surely be the best known and loved of all the Psalms. It embodies what particularly attracts us to these ancient poems—and perhaps also makes us a bit wary of digging too deeply into them. After all, part of its appeal is its immediacy. It needs little or no explanation. Its imagery draws us right in. Its message of trust and assurance allows us to draw a deep breath even in the most difficult of moments. Why *study* it? Why not leave well enough alone?

For one thing, many of the Psalms are *not* as direct and accessible as Psalm 23; in fact, they can be profoundly puzzling to modern readers. But even this psalm can raise questions for us, particularly if we encounter it in an unfamiliar translation. And there are layers of meaning under some of its well known expressions that can enrich our reading when we learn about them. Of course, what most of us *don't* want in a book about the Psalms is to be told, "Say, that psalm you've loved so much for so long—well, you've got it all wrong."

Draw a deep breath, then. That is not what this Conversation with Scripture aims to do. The Psalms are poems.

And, as with poetry in general, it is possible for their meanings to change and deepen with time. In fact, it is inevitable, for any time we take a text out of its historical context of culture and language and read it in a different culture more than two thousand years later, it *will* seem a bit different. (For that matter, as writers in general can attest, there is no guarantee that any writing will mean exactly the same thing even to contemporary readers as it did to its writer.)

Even in Psalm 23, there are things worth pondering. The assumption in this book is that we will be reading the Psalms in the New Revised Standard Version (NRSV). One notices very quickly that this is not identical to the most familiar English versions, whether that of the King James Version or the version found in the Book of Common Prayer. But even before we take up those differences, there are some things worth thinking about.

For one thing, why "shepherd"? It is an image of some power for modern readers—and yet fairly remote for most of us, since we are likely to be city-dwellers with little direct experience of sheep or those who tend them. The ancient world, where cities were smaller and more integrated with the countryside, was quite different in that regard. This is one part of the explanation. But "shepherd" also had a further dimension. In ancient Israel (and Greece, too, for that matter) it was a metaphor for "king" (e.g., Ezek 34). This seemed important enough to early Latin translators that they began their version of the psalm *Dominus regit me:* "The Lord rules me" or "guides me." If you know Latin, you will detect an echo here of the noun *rex*, "king."

Part of what the shepherd image conveys, then, is God's *power* to protect and nourish the sheep. The psalmist gives us a quite vivid image of how this looks from the perspective of sheep in the field— of us, the readers, *as if* we were sheep in the field:

> The LORD is my shepherd, I shall not want.
>> He makes me lie down in green pastures;
> he leads me beside still waters;
>> he restores my soul. (23:1–3a)

But wait a moment! Do sheep have souls? Well, yes, from the ancient perspective. In English, "soul" can sound like a specifically spiritual component of the human being, but the ancient Hebrew word behind it meant something more like "life force." Restoring one's soul meant a renewal of energy and hope for life—that deep breath that releases us from anxiety and care and often comes precisely from having enough to eat and drink, some protection from danger, and the beauty of the natural world surrounding us. All this the poet has managed to convey in just four lines of verse.

But then we run into an issue of translation when we read:

> He leads me in right paths
>   for his name's sake. (23:3b–c)

Why not the more familiar "paths of righteousness"? One basic question for translators is whether to represent each individual word in a phrase ("paths of righteousness," in this case) or try to capture the meaning of the phrase as a whole ("right paths"). Different translators make different decisions. In this case, the NRSV translators may have thought that "paths of righteousness" was too narrow, too much like "obeying all the rules." The Hebrew phrase actually includes every aspect of choice involved in leading a generous and humane kind of life. Either way, the line is still saying that God leads us in the way we ought and need to go, the way that contributes to the well-being of our lives and of the world around us, the way that will bring us home.

We may have a similar question about "the darkest valley" as an alternative to "the valley of the shadow of death." Here, the NRSV translation is based on another kind of linguistic consideration, having to do with historical change *within* the Hebrew language. It is now clear that, early in the history of Hebrew, the phrase in question would indeed have meant something like "valley of deep darkness." On the other hand, by the second century BCE, when the ancient Greek translation of the Psalms was made, it had come to mean something more like "valley of the shadow of death," which makes the threat more explicit. Choosing which way to translate it is difficult because we don't know when Psalm 23 was written—early or late. Either image is vivid. Either is possible. Feel free to take your choice!

The psalm ends with a festive banquet. We can think of the enemies as looking on from a distance and eating their hearts out—a thought with parallels in other psalms, which often take a certain pleasure in the prospect of vengeance. But you are free to picture, instead, a time when human beings will be reconciled with one another at the banquet of the age to come. Even if we could be sure which meaning the original author had in mind, we live in *our* world and may find that we embrace a different vision for the future.

The ancient Greek translators even found a further implication in this passage. The Hebrew phrase that lies behind "my cup overflows" is actually not quite grammatical, which could suggest that some mistake has crept into it. The Greek translators, whether they had a different Hebrew text or were just trying to make sense of the same one that we know, produced something that we can translate into English as "Your cup renders one utterly intoxicated." They were reading it as a reference to mystical experience, for which intoxication is an age-old metaphor. (Many modern readers have encountered it in the poetry of Rumi.)

Finally, the banquet broadens out into hope for a life of "goodness and mercy." And the psalm ends with a reference to the temple: "I shall dwell in the house of the LORD my whole life long." As we shall see, this focus on the temple is common to a great many of the Psalms, where it provides an image of particular intimacy with God. We have reached "home."

Psalm 23, like the Psalms in general, engages us in a very direct and immediate way. We read scripture for all sorts of reasons: we get interested in the stories; we ponder the commandments; we get advice from the wisdom literature; we explore theological questions. We study and reflect on what the other scriptures say *to* us. The Psalms, on the other hand, insist on placing themselves in our own mouths. They ask to be read aloud or, better, sung. They make us speak in the first person—"I" and "we." They claim, more often than not, to represent *our* side of the conversation with God, to give voice to our own joys and sorrows, our own fears and hopes. And they achieve this in language that is deeply poetic and directly accessible. It is what gives them so much power. It also makes them well worth digging more deeply into.

CHAPTER ONE

"Praise God in His Sanctuary…"

Songs for the Temple

The English word "psalm" comes from the Greek *psalmos*, meaning "a song with plucked accompaniment" on a stringed instrument such as a harp. It is the name that the ancient Greek translators of the Hebrew Scriptures gave to the poems in this book. The book's Hebrew name is *Tehillim*, meaning "praises," even though not all the Psalms fall into that precise category. Perhaps the Greek translators were looking for a more neutral term to cover all these poems. In English, the word "psalm" refers specifically to the poems in this book, but also to other poems, usually religious, that resemble them in some way.

A related word is "psalter," meaning a collection of psalms. Anglicans know the word from its use in the Book of Common Prayer. Then, just to confuse things, there is yet another English word from this same Greek source: "psaltery." It refers to an ancient musical instrument, probably one with strings of graduated length like a harp. It occurred in older English translations of the Psalms, but has dropped out of most recent ones.

The book of Psalms is an anthology, gathering together poems written over a long period of time. If you read it

"psalm"—a religious poem such as the Biblical psalms
"psalter"—a collection of such poems
"psaltery"—an ancient stringed instrument similar to a harp

right through, you will find that it lacks continuity, as is typical of anthologies. One consequence of this is that we will draw our materials for study from here and there in the Psalter, bringing together psalms that have related themes. Each section will begin by listing the psalms under discussion in it, and it will be a good idea to read them before reading the section itself. Some sections will also include suggestions about other, related psalms to read afterward.

The poems themselves are of various kinds, including hymns of praise (the focus of our Chapter 3), laments and thanksgivings and expressions of trust (Chapter 4), and thoughtful reflections on life and faith (Chapter 5). Some were meant for public liturgies; some convey the prayers of the king or focus on community concerns; others express more private thoughts and needs. They were written over a long period of time. Some may go back as far as the time of David (around 1000 BCE) or even before, and a good many stem from the time when Israel and Judah were independent kingdoms (the ninth to the sixth centuries). Others date later, to the time of the Babylonian Exile (586–538 BCE) or even afterward—to the time when returned exiles were gradually rebuilding Jerusalem under Persian rule. Texts from different eras were gradually brought together into small collections, which in turn were gathered together, rearranged, and edited into our existing Book of Psalms no later than the fourth century BCE.

What inspired and guided the collecting process was the usefulness of these poems in the temple at Jerusalem, the heart of Israelite worship from the time when King David seized the city from its original Jebusite inhabitants and his son Solomon built the first great temple there in the tenth century BCE. Solomon's Temple was destroyed by the Babylonians, but the returning exiles rebuilt it. This new structure, referred to as the "Second Temple," went through several phases of reworking and enhancement, concluding with a sumptuous reconstruction of it by Herod the Great at the turn of the eras. The resulting edifice was famous throughout the ancient Mediterranean world before its destruction by the Romans in 70 CE.

The Psalter was given its existing form for use in the Second Temple. We will return to the question of how this mass of poems was brought together and edited at the end of this chapter. But, first, we take a look at what some of the psalms tell us about the temple and its worship, particularly the part that music and song played in it.

A Temple for Singing Praises: Psalm 150

Psalm 150, coming as it does at the end of the Psalter, brings the whole collection to a celebratory conclusion, a kind of shout of joy. And it gives us some sense of the music that would have accompanied these texts. On high feast days, at least, it was loud—a grand affair combining choruses of singers and an orchestra of stringed instruments such as lyres and harps, flutes, trumpets, and percussion. This was very different from the music used subsequently in ancient synagogues and churches. Traditionally, synagogues allowed only vocal music, and this may have been at least partly to underline the fact that the synagogue did not claim to be on a par with the Jerusalem temple. Early Christians followed the same usage. But temple music pulled out all the stops—to speak figuratively, for the organ had not yet been invented—and the fact that the temple was built around a succession of open courtyards must have made the sheer volume of sound both desirable and necessary. (For a similar description of the temple music, see Psalm 98.)

Temple music, on high feast days, was a grand affair combining choruses of singers and an orchestra of stringed instruments, flutes, trumpets, and percussion.

The temple had a uniquely important role in the religion of ancient Israel. It was *the* sanctuary, the one place where sacrifice was to be offered to God. Its uniqueness reflected that of the One God. To be there was to stand in God's presence. Psalm 150 expresses its importance succinctly:

Praise God in his sanctuary;
  praise him in his mighty firmament! (150:1)

There was a direct correspondence between the sanctuary on earth and God's throne in the firmament—the crystalline dome described in the account of creation as forming the sky (Gen 1:6–8). Just as the One God had only one true residence in heaven, there could be only one temple on earth. Synagogues, by contrast, which probably first came into existence during and after the Exile, were community meeting places for the study of Torah and the saying of prayers. Only in the temple did worshipers expect to come so immediately and directly into God's presence.

The author of Psalm 150 conveys this by drawing us into the experience of actually being at the sanctuary, amid what must have seemed an almost deafening volume of sound. The psalm serves as a virtual embodiment of the celebration itself. It does not spend much time saying anything *about* God. The reference to the firmament reminds us that God is creator as well as ruler of the universe. The passing reference to "mighty deeds" and "surpassing greatness" is sufficient to remind the congregation of stories they already know. The real emphasis is simply on summoning the assembled people (and the full orchestra with all its gleefully enumerated instruments) to join in the praises. Finally, in a move that is not uncommon in the Psalms, our poet enthusiastically widens this invitation to include the whole created order: "Let everything that breathes praise the LORD!" The temple is, in effect, the center both for Israel's worship and for that of the whole creation. Reason enough to fill it with music—and, no doubt, dance as well, as we shall see in some other psalms.

Israel's Temple: Psalms 135, 149

First and foremost, however, the temple was the shrine of *Israel's* particular, covenanted relationship with its God. Accordingly, most psalms focus more specifically on the concerns of the nation that came together in Jerusalem for worship. Compare, for example, **Psalm 149**, which begins, rather like Psalm 150, with a summons to the assembled multitude to join in God's praise:

> Let Israel be glad in its Maker;
>> let the children of Zion rejoice in their King.
> Let them praise his name with dancing,
>> making melody to him with tambourine and lyre. (149:2–3)

The poet goes on to describe Israel with two significant terms: "the humble"—not so much a matter of attitude as of the sometimes marginal existence of a relatively small nation surrounded by rivals, some of them larger and more powerful—and also as "the faithful," to signify that commitment to God was the foundation of their victory against such odds. The worshipping community is a threatened people relying on God for survival. To be sure, there were times when Israel dominated other nations in its neighborhood; but it was never completely free from anxiety.

The psalmist then describes in some detail what this victory will mean. It will be a military triumph:

> to execute vengeance on the nations
>   and punishment on the peoples,
> to bind their kings with fetters
>   and their nobles with chains of iron. (149:7–8)

The psalm pictures a time when the threat will be past and "the faithful" will "sing for joy on their couches," as they recline at a victory banquet. Even then, however, the psalmist wants them to keep "a two-edged sword in their hands" for the next round of national defense.

The martial element in the Psalms is an accurate reflection of the times when they were written and could hardly have been avoided in a sanctuary that was, for all its claims to God's universality, the temple of a particular nation.

It should be no surprise that this martial element is a repeated motif in the Psalms. It is an accurate reflection of the times when they were written and could hardly have been avoided in poetry created for a sanctuary that was, for all its interest in God's universality, also the temple of a particular nation and of its God, the guarantor of its national existence. The tension between the particular and the universal pervades the Psalter as a whole.

Psalm 135 offers a treatment of the martial theme more nuanced than that of Psalm 149. It, too, begins with an exhortation:

> Praise the LORD!
>   Praise the name of the LORD;
>   give praise, O servants of the LORD,
> you that stand in the house of the LORD,
>   in the courts of the house of our God. (135:1–2)

Those who "stand in the house of God," will have been Israelites, for no one else was admitted to the sanctuary. Gentiles had to remain outside a certain perimeter, marked in Herod's Temple with inscriptions warning that transgressors would be executed. The reason was a concern that non-Israelites, whether intentionally or from ignorance, would pollute the sanctuary and make it displeasing to God.

When the psalm appeals, then, to people standing in the temple itself and its inner courts, it is calling on Israelites. They are to praise God because "he is gracious"—gracious specifically to "Jacob," the patriarch who was renamed "Israel" and became the ancestor of the whole nation (Gen 32:22–32). They are to praise God also in terms of God's power in nature. The psalmist associates God particularly with storm clouds and lightning—something found in other psalms as well. It was an obvious enough choice of symbol in a region with intense thunderstorms; the Greeks and Romans, like many Ancient Near Eastern peoples, associated their chief god with the power of the lightning bolt. This was not a simple *identification* of God with the powers of nature. It was a metaphor that conveyed a sense of God's pervasive power.

Psalm 135 next moves on to recall highlights of the Exodus, when God favored Israel by punishing or destroying their enemies, both the imperial power of pharaonic Egypt and the local powers of Canaan, whose names are recited like an incantation:

> Sihon, king of the Amorites,
> and Og, king of Bashan,
> and all the kingdoms of Canaan (135:11)

(This list appears again in Psalm 136.) But the poet's attention turns quickly to theological reflection. What do these victories mean? Not that God is violent, but that the God of Israel is a living God, active in the world, in contrast to the gods of the nations who are no more alive than the images that represent them:

> They have mouths, but they do not speak;
> they have eyes, but they do not see. . . . (135:16)

The sanctuary in Jerusalem was the place where, above all, people would be conscious of this contrast between Israel's God and the gods of other nations. Indeed, the Jerusalem temple was an ongoing source of perplexity to other ancient peoples because it contained no cult image of the God worshipped there. Such images (or "idols," as scripture calls them) were the norm everywhere else. Israel was unique in banishing them from its temple. The Holy of Holies, the innermost and most sacred space in the sanctuary, did hold two images, but they represented not God, but God's servants the cherubim. Along with them, the space contained, in the time of the First Temple, the Ark of the Covenant, ancient symbol of God's power in battle. In the Second Temple, the Ark having been lost, it stood empty. The temple was the concrete expression of the Ten Commandments' ban on making images of God.

Finally, Psalm 135 concludes with four exhortations to praise, naming four different groups that participated in the temple's worship: the house of Israel (i.e., the citizen body of the nation understood as sharing a common descent from Jacob), the house of Aaron (the family that supplied priests for the Temple), the house of Levi (other members of the priestly tribe who filled other offices in the Temple, including that of musicians), and those "who fear the LORD." This last group was probably composed of particularly devout worshippers. For the whole nation to join in God's praise required only the involvement of the first three groups. But there were also people distinguished by their intense devotion, forming an ongoing presence in the sanctuary. (We read of two such figures in the latter days of the Second Temple—Simeon and Anna—in Luke 2:25–38.) A number of psalms take account of their presence and some, particularly those called "wisdom psalms," may well represent some of their perspectives.

> *Four different groups made up the assembly in the Temple complex: the house of Israel (i.e., the nation as a whole), the house of Aaron (the family that supplied priests for the Temple), the house of Levi (other members of the priestly tribe who served as temple musicians among other roles), and those "who fear the LORD."*

The Psalms thus draw on the full variety of perspectives present among the worshippers. Some are quite frankly political or military in focus; others, even while maintaining this element, are also beginning to think, in more reflective terms, about how and why God is radically different from the gods of the nations. Yet others reveal the particular spiritual longings of the devout.

A National and a Universal God:
Psalms 29, 68, 82

There is some diversity of thought in the Hebrew Scriptures on the topic of God—and particularly in the Psalms. Israel was surrounded by other nations with their individual divinities. One strand of thinking did not deny the reality of these other gods, but simply subordinated them to the God of Israel. **Psalm 29** may be one of the oldest poems in the Psalter, for it has elements that relate it to literature of the second millennium BCE found at the ancient city of Ugarit on the Syrian coast. It begins by telling the other gods to "ascribe to the LORD the glory of his name." NRSV is a little misleading in its translation "heavenly beings." It gives a more literal translation of the Hebrew in the footnote: "sons of gods," which represents a Hebrew idiom meaning, roughly, "beings belonging to the category of gods." This reflects the ancient polytheistic tradition of a heavenly council made up of a variety of gods, sometimes cooperating, sometimes working against one another. One might think of the behavior of the Greek gods in Homer.

The poet of Psalm 29, however, is very clear that these divinities are all subordinate to the God of Israel. The psalm then goes on to celebrate God in imagery of thunder and lightning:

> The voice of the LORD is over the waters:
>> the God of glory thunders,
>> the Lord, over mighty waters. (29:3)

Our poet evokes a scene of vast destruction:

> The voice of the LORD breaks the cedars;
>> the LORD breaks the cedars of Lebanon. (29:5)

The damage done in the north, on Mount Lebanon, is repeated to the south, where "the LORD shakes the wilderness of Kadesh." The oaks, too—perhaps to the east where Bashan was famous for these trees—writhe and are stripped bare. But then we are transported in an instant from forest to sanctuary: "and in his temple all say, 'Glory!'"

This last line may seem abrupt, but it captures the essential continuity between the temple, the throne of God in heaven, and the activity of God throughout the world. It is like Isaiah's vision in the temple, where he saw "the Lord sitting on a throne, high and lofty," and surrounded by the seraphim who sang "Holy, holy, holy is the LORD of hosts." (Isa 6:1–5) Just as we saw in Psalm 150, to be in the temple is to be at God's heavenly throne:

> The LORD sits enthroned over the flood:
>   the LORD sits enthroned as king forever.
> May the LORD give strength to his people!
>   May the LORD bless his people with peace! (29:10–11)

Other gods may exist, but none dares challenge the God of Israel.

Psalm 82 constructs another scene of Israel's God standing in the council of gods. But, at first, there is no suggestion of any distinction in power. Instead, we have a kind of courtroom drama. God, as one member of the council, accuses the others of failing in their duty to maintain the world through justice:

> "How long will you judge unjustly
>   and show partiality to the wicked? *Selah*
> Give justice to the weak and the orphan;
>   maintain the right of the lowly and the destitute." (82:2–3)

The other gods are dismayed and driven into disarray by this exposure of their wickedness. The psalmist provides a vivid description of the scene and its consequences:

> They have neither knowledge nor understanding,
>   they walk around in darkness;
>   all the foundations of the earth are shaken. (82:5)

When the gods are proven guilty, they are shown to be ignorant and blind. The consequence is that "all the foundations of the earth are shaken."

God then seizes the moment to pronounce judgment on the other gods, who become henceforth subject to death:

> I say, "You are gods,
>   children of the Most High, all of you;
> nevertheless, you shall die like mortals,
>   and fall like any prince." (82:6–7)

There is at least a hint here that these other gods are his own off-spring, "children of the Most High." Or perhaps *El Elyon*, the Most High God, was conceived, in the remote past, as a universal god above the contests of other gods. In any case, it is clear who comes out of this drama vindicated. Note how the psalmist concludes the story. Since Israel's God has triumphed in court against the other gods, the psalm ends by praying:

> Rise up, O God, judge the earth;
> for all the nations belong to you! (82:8)

We are witnessing, in mythological terms, the moment when Israel's God shifts from being one among many to being the only God. And this is achieved not by warfare, but by practicing justice.

This did not mean that warfare was being dropped from God's function. The editors of the Psalter brought together a broad array of materials and did not always try to harmonize their perspectives. An extremely warlike version of God among other heavenly powers is found in **Psalm 68**. But this time the other powers are clearly and firmly subordinate; they are God's army:

> With mighty chariotry, twice ten thousand,
> thousands upon thousands,
> the Lord came from Sinai into the holy place. (68:17)

Psalm 68 is a poetic master-piece, however uncomfortable its topic may make us. One can at least sympathize with it as the victory song of a community endangered by powerful opponents and delivered from destruction only by their defeat.

These chariots are not land-bound vehicles with human charioteers. It would have been a rough road from Sinai to the sanctuary! They are heavenly chariots driven by a host of heavenly beings, whom we may legitimately, in this context, call "angels" rather than "gods."

Psalm 68 is a masterpiece of poetry, however uncomfortable the topic may make us. There is plenty of bloodshed in it with God shattering "the heads of his enemies, the hairy crown of those who walk in their guilty ways." If we are to understand or sympathize with it, we have to recognize it as the victory song of a community endangered by powerful opponents and delivered from destruction only by their defeat.

The description of God in Psalm 68 is similar to what we saw in Psalms 29 and 135. Storm imagery appears in 68:7–10, but with the difference that the downpour of rain is now seen as producing not only destruction, but also the positive result of abundant fresh pasturage. And, as in Psalm 82, God's true strength lies not in sheer force but in deep commitment to justice:

Father of orphans and protector of widows
    is God in his holy habitation. (68:5)

This does not alter the fact that the poem is celebrating a real experience of war. The triumphant warrior God leads a train of captives to Mount Zion (v. 18). Those who fled will be chased down, brought back, and slaughtered (vv. 21–23). In an almost cinematic shift of scene, we turn from the bloodshed to see the women at home bedecking themselves with the spoil till they look like iridescent rock doves (the same species as the modern pigeon) (vv. 12–13). Part of the greatness of this poet's achievement is the ability to wed graphic terror to the almost inexpressible relief of the people who are thereby spared the same fate at the hands of their enemies and who express their joy in procession to the sanctuary:

the singers in front, the musicians last,
    between them girls playing tambourines. . . . (68:25)

while the leaders of the southernmost and northernmost tribes, representing the full reach of the nation, follow along, as well (27).

The emotional necessity of such rejoicing is evident, and its ethical danger is also clearly on display here. There is a sharp, seemingly self-evident distinction between the wicked "them" and the righteous "us" (68:2–3). Even more telling, the enemy are reduced to the level of beasts, making their slaughter seem less problematic; they become "the wild animals that live among the reeds, the herd of bulls with the calves of the peoples" (30). We might wish that the scriptures in general or the Psalms in particular would provide us with less complex materials for the life of faith. But, truth to tell, human life in itself is not free of such complexity, and it is not inappropriate to find ourselves confronted with the conflict between celebrating triumph after great danger and the slippery slope that can lead to the dehumanization of our enemies—particularly when it is framed for us in poetry of such power.

We will find again and again that the Psalter offers us a broad range of human experience and perspective as materiel for constructing the life of faith. The perfect simplicity of Psalm 23 stands alongside other psalms that we may find we cannot take on as our own utterance without significant reservations. The Psalter is, after all, framed as expressing *human* thoughts, not, on the whole, those of God. This will inevitably include some thoughts that we normally censor. In fact, the Psalms stand in sharp contrast to our frequent presupposition that prayer should present only our best face to God. That more polite model of prayer does not always incorporate our full humanity or push us toward such deep self-examination.

The Temple and the World: Psalms 47, 87

Even Psalm 68 has a certain sense that God is God of the world, not just of the nation. It re-emphasizes the connection between God and Israel (68:35), but it also summons "the kingdoms of the earth" to "sing praises to the Lord" (32). Perhaps it is only inviting them to accept tributary status—as the preceding verse could suggest:

> Let bronze be brought from Egypt;
>   let Ethiopia hasten to stretch out its hands to God. (68:31)

Nonetheless, it cannot quite avoid the implications of God's universality. Since God was Creator of the whole world and, indeed, the only true God, there had to be some way to think of the temple as center for the worship not just of one nation but of all humanity. We see evidence of this thinking in some other psalms that stand alongside the more specifically nationalist strand of thinking we noted above.

Psalm 47 begins by emphasizing the centrality of Israel. Even though it summons all the peoples to celebrate God's kingship, it cites, as evidence of God's power, the triumph of Israel over its enemies:

> He subdued peoples under us,
>   and nations under our feet. (47:3)

The conclusion of the psalm, however, implies that one could ultimately think of other nations as joining in the worship of the temple:

God is king over the nations;
  God sits on his holy throne.
The princes of the peoples gather
  as the people of the God of Abraham.
For the shields of the earth belong to God:
  he is highly exalted. (47:8–9)

There is still a clear priority for Israel and for Jerusalem:

God has gone up with a shout,
  the LORD with the sound of a trumpet. (47:5)

"Gone up," that is, to the sanctuary, for in the Psalms that is the usual implication of the language of "going up." Yet, the focus on the temple does not mean the exclusion of all others, for "the shields of the earth" all belong to God. God is, in the fundamental sense, God even of those who do not yet know it.

> *God is, in the fundamental sense, God even of those who do not yet know it.*

  This belief in God's universal authority meant that there was always at least a hope that humanity would be fully united in worship at Jerusalem. **Psalm 87** affords a beautiful and moving celebration of this hope that begins with the praise of Zion:

On the holy mount stands the city he founded:
  the LORD loves the gates of Zion
  more than all the dwellings of Jacob.
Glorious things are spoken of you, O city of God. (87:1–3)

But then it goes on to claim not just Israel, but all the nations of the world as natives of this place: Rahab (probably a reference to Egypt), Babylon, Philistia, Tyre, Ethiopia. "'This one was born there,' they say." Note that the first three names represent hereditary enemies of Israel. It might occur to us to ask whether this refers not to native populations, but to Jewish people who were living as resident aliens in these places. But this possibility is contradicted by the psalm's conclusion, which speaks of "the peoples":

And of Zion it shall be said,
  "This one and that one were born in it":
  for the Most High himself will establish it.

17

The LORD records, as he registers the peoples,
　　"This one was born there." (87:5–6)

And this gathering of the nations is presented not as conquest, but as a celebration of Zion's capacity to embrace the world:

Singers and dancers alike say,
　　"All my springs are in you." (87:7)

The words are allusive, which makes them all the more powerful. What are these springs? Places of origin? Places of refreshment? Places where humans find their true lives? Yes, all of these and more. They sum up the life-giving generosity of God, extending potentially to all humanity.

Zion's Temple: Psalms 26, 27, 48

However wide the temple's reach might be, it still remained intimately connected with the place where it stood—Jerusalem, yes, but more particularly Mount Zion, the ridge where it was constructed and re-constructed over time. Zion is a recurrent theme in the Psalms.

In the days of the First Temple, some even argued that God's residence in the sanctuary made Zion impregnable. Not all agreed. Isaiah seemed to embrace this idea in his oracle about Sennacherib (Isa 37:21–38), but Jeremiah rejected it emphatically (6:1–30). And, in fact, Zion did fall to the Chaldeans in Jeremiah's time. The idea is at least implied in **Psalm 48**. To praise Zion and to celebrate God become virtually the same thing here:

Great is the LORD and greatly to be praised,
　　in the city of our God.
His holy mountain, beautiful in elevation,
　　is the joy of all the earth,
Mount Zion, in the far north,
　　the city of the great King.
Within its citadels God
　　has shown himself a sure defense. (48:1–3)

(The odd reference to Zion as being "in the far north" seems to be a borrowing from Canaanite mythology, which located the mountain of the gods in the north.)

The psalm goes on to recount an idealized history. Whenever foreign powers have gathered to attack Zion, they have been thrown into a panic and taken to flight, scattered by God's might "as when an east wind shatters the ships of Tarshish" (v. 7). (Tarshish, in the Iberian peninsula, gave its name to the largest type of cargo vessel.) One wonders if this psalm may have been written to celebrate deliverance from just such a menace, perhaps the very assault of Sennacherib that Isaiah prophesied about (2 Kings 18–19); but it remained in use long after Jerusalem fell to the Babylonians because, even though its military guarantee had proved wrong, it celebrated the sense of God's immediate presence—the supreme religious value that people sought and found in the temple.

However wide the temple's reach might be, it remained intimately connected with the place where it stood—Jerusalem, yes, but more particularly Mount Zion, the ridge where it was constructed and re-constructed over time.

In **Psalm 27**, trust in the Lord is expressed partly in terms of a longing to be in the temple. The psalmist begins by asserting confidence in God:

> The LORD is my light and my salvation;
>> whom shall I fear?
> The LORD is the stronghold of my life;
>> of whom shall I be afraid? (27:1)

This sense of attachment to God offers hope in the midst of present dangers, but even more than that it expresses a longing for the beloved presence:

> One thing I asked of the LORD,
>> that I will seek after:
> to live in the house of the LORD
>> all the days of my life,
> to behold the beauty of the Lord,
>> and to inquire in his temple. (27:4)

This is a prescription for a life immersed in God's grace.

Psalm 26 expresses a similar deep affection for the sanctuary:

> I wash my hands in innocence,
>> and go around your altar, O LORD,

> singing aloud a song of thanksgiving,
>> and telling all your wondrous deeds.
> O LORD, I love the house in which you dwell,
>> and the place where your glory abides. (26:6–8)

The expression of love may not be entirely without self-interest here. This psalm opens with a request for vindication and may have served as part of a rite by which one sought to clear oneself of a false accusation that could not be conclusively disproved. The centrality of Zion, however, and love for its sanctuary are themes that we see again and again in our reading of the Psalms.

Assembling the Psalter: Hints from Titles

Since the Psalter includes poems composed over a long period of time and probably in a variety of places, one wonders how it came together into the version we now have. No doubt much of the answer has to do with accidents of preservation and loss over centuries of sometimes disastrous history. A few psalms may be very old indeed. As we noted, Psalm 29 uses imagery more common in the second millennium BCE than later. At the other end of the time-spectrum, Psalm 137, with its reference to exile in Babylon, cannot date from before the 580s BCE. In some psalms, the high priest seems to be the leading figure of the community, with no reference to a king. These would date still later— to the period of Persian rule. There is nothing, however, to suggest that the psalms accumulated in order of composition, with the oldest first. It is more likely that the final editors of the Psalter found several existing collections, which they combined and adapted and to which they added some materials of their own day.

One clue, though not always easy to interpret, is the titles that appear at the beginning of many psalms. Beginning with Psalm 3 there is a long series of psalms connected with the name of David. The titles of Psalms 3–41 and 51–70 almost all make some reference to David, and they may have constituted one or two early collections. Indeed, there is a brief note at the end of Psalm 72 (itself attributed to Solomon) that says, "The prayers of David son of Jesse are ended."

This does not mean that David necessarily wrote this whole collection—or, for that matter, any individual psalm in it. He was thought of, early on, as the archetypal singer and player of the harp. (His music helped calm King Saul when he was tormented by mental and emotional distress, 1 Sam 16:14–23). This made him the ideal authority to stand behind such a collection. In a similar way, the whole book of Proverbs was attributed to the archetypal wise man, Solomon, even though chapters 30 and 31 were admittedly composed by other people.

> *David was thought of, early on, as the archetypal singer and player of the harp, which made him the ideal authority to stand behind such a collection.*

Some psalm titles speak of specific events in David's life such as his flight from his son Absalom (3), or the time when he was betrayed by the people of Ziph (54). But these notes may well have been added as the collection was built up simply because these psalms seemed appropriate to the occasion. More commonly, the titles tell us not about the origin of a psalm, but about specifics of performance. Thus, Psalm 4 is to be accompanied by stringed instruments, but Psalm 5 by flutes. Many of the titles begin with "To the leader," i.e. the musician in charge. Some tell us the tune for singing the psalm, such as "The Deer of the Dawn" (22) or "The Dove on the Far-off Terebinths" (56). Others may give other sorts of musical information: *Sheminith* (Ps 6), for example, means "eighth" and could refer to a specific musical mode. (Whereas modern Western music relies mainly on just two modes, major and minor, ancient music had eight.)

Another musical direction, the obscure term "Selah," appears in the body of psalms. Its literal meaning is something like "lift up," and while its meaning in this context is obscure, many believe that it marked a place for an instrumental interlude. At Ps 9:6, it is joined by the even more uncertain term "Higgaion." Most English translations have wisely left these terms in Hebrew, since we know so little about them. A few other words, such as "Shiggaion" (7), "Miktam" (16), and "Maskil" (32) may have indicated particular types of psalms, but we have no certainty as to what they meant, either.

Titles identify some other groupings of psalms with the guilds of levitical singers in the temple. A group of these (42–49), attributed to the Korahites, is found in the middle of the Psalms of David, followed by another (Ps 50) described as a Psalm of Asaph. More Psalms of Asaph follow (73–83) and then more Korahite psalms (84–85, 87–88) and one of Ethan the Ezrahite (89). All these were the names of families who provided music in the temple.

Psalms after 89 have fewer titles attached to them apart from Psalms 120–35, which carry the title "Song of Ascents." These may well have been collected for the use of pilgrims on their way to Jerusalem. Of the remaining psalms, one is attributed to Moses (90), one to Solomon (127), and several to David, but the titles in this last portion of the Psalter suggest less pre-existing organization of the materials.

Assembling the Psalter: Hints from Language: Psalms 14, 53, 114

A few other groups of psalms are distinguished by linguistic considerations. Several groupings are referred to as "hallels" from their use of a Hebrew phrase that has entered the English language as "Hallelujah" or (via Greek and Latin) "Alleluia." The NRSV translates it as "Praise the LORD." One such group—Psalms 113–18—is often called the "Egyptian Hallel" and was probably formed as an element in the rites of Passover, a function it still serves. **Psalm 114**, in just eight verses, brilliantly condenses the whole story of the Exodus, including the wilderness wandering and the entry into Canaan, to a series of brief images. It begins by linking the start and ending of the story closely together:

> When Israel went out from Egypt,
>   the house of Jacob from a people of strange language,
> Judah became God's sanctuary,
>   Israel his dominion. (114:1–2)

This covers the whole story from Exodus to Joshua—and even the founding of the temple—in four lines! We find a similar juxtaposition of earlier and later moments of the story in the next verse where the crossing of the Red Sea is coupled with the crossing of the Jordan. Attached to these partings of the waters is earthquake imagery, but, by comparing the shaking of mountains and hills to the bounding of lambs, the poet gives even an earthquake an element of joy and delight. Only in the conclusion does the trembling become a sign of awe in the presence of a life-giving God who brings forth water in the desert:

> Tremble, O earth, at the presence of the LORD,
>   at the presence of the God of Jacob,

who turns the rock into a pool of water,
the flint into a spring of water. (114:7–8)

The reference here is to the miracle of water struck from the rock in the desert wandering (Exod 17:1–7).

Another such collection, the "Great Hallel," includes Psalms 135–36, which also recount the events of the Exodus and entry into Canaan. They form a significant element in the synagogue's daily morning service, as does the "Little Hallel" that consists of Psalms 146–50. These psalms also serve to bring the Psalter to a close with rejoicing. This final grouping of psalms may well have been created deliberately by the editors of the whole Psalter for this very purpose.

One final (and much less obvious) indication of sources cuts across some of the lines we have already drawn. For the most part, the Psalter freely uses the Hebrew *name* of God, which is written with Hebrew letters corresponding to YHWH in Roman characters. The name, however, has long since ceased to be pronounced; in reading the Hebrew Scriptures, one substitutes the Hebrew *adonai*, a form of a word meaning "lord." This name is represented in NRSV by "LORD," using small caps to make it distinct. Psalms 42–83, however, tend to avoid the name altogether and prefer the word *elohim*, "God." For this reason, these psalms are sometimes spoken of as the "Elohistic Psalter." They may well represent yet another early collection, perhaps connected originally with the northern Kingdom of Israel, where other evidence also suggests a preference for this terminology. Since Christians tend to use "Lord" and "God" interchangeably, we may not take much notice of this shift. But it has produced the slightly odd result of two almost identical psalms, **14 and 53**, distinguished from each other by little except this issue of vocabulary.

Comparison of the two will make the point very quickly. The first substantive difference, found in verse 2 of each psalm, is the choice of "the LORD" in 14 and "God" in 53. The only major difference after that is the way each finishes out the couplet beginning with "There they shall be in great terror . . ." (verse 5). It is clearly a case of a single original composition that was edited and handed down separately in two different collections.

Some readers will have little interest in probing the past of the Psalter. Still, we sometimes find odd bits of information, surprising

> Throughout the Psalter, we find odd bits of information, contradictions, parallelisms, and peculiar juxtapositions that pique our interest. Often, some consideration of how these poems came to be arranged as they are can be illuminating.

contradictions (or, alternatively, unexpected parallelisms), and peculiar juxtapositions that pique our interest. Consideration of how these poems came to be collected and arranged can be illuminating then. How else, for example, would we make sense of the almost perfect similarity between Psalms 14 and 53? Or the common style and language of Psalms 146–50?

One of the final steps in the process of collecting and editing, it seems, was to place Psalm 1, the praise of the upright person, as the prologue to the whole collection. The editors also divided their new anthology into five books, probably to echo the number of the Books of Moses, the Torah:

Book I	Ps 1–41
Book II	Ps 42–72
Book III	Ps 73–89
Book IV	Ps 90–106
Book V	Ps 107–50

Each of the first four books ends with a short doxology. Three of these four fit their context well enough that the reader might not notice them as something distinct. But the one that falls at the end of Psalm 89 seems very odd in relation to the body of that psalm and can only be understood as a conclusion to the whole of Book III. Psalm 150 serves, in its own way, as a kind of concluding doxology for the Psalter as a whole.

For the most part, we read the psalms as individual compositions. But, taken as a group, they preserve a broad assortment of perspectives—too broad to be reduced easily to agreement. The editors may have nudged them at times into greater conformity with each other and with their own religious understanding. Still, the interplay created when their differences are brought together within a single collection is part of what renders the whole Psalter so rich a text of faith and spirituality. It makes little effort to present a fully coherent account of theology or spirituality; instead, it provides a poetic anthology built up through a long history of worship and focused by the privileged place of Zion's sanctuary in the religion of ancient Israel.

Continuing the Conversation:

An annotated Bible or, for more extensive comment, a one-volume Bible commentary are excellent aids for studying the Bible. Two suggestions:

The New Oxford Annotated Bible, NRSV with Apocrypha, 4th ed. (New York: Oxford University Press, 2010)

HarperCollins Bible Commentary, rev. ed. (New York: HarperCollins, 2000)

On the centrality of Jerusalem in history, see Samuel Sebag Montefiore, *Jerusalem: The Biography* (New York: Alfred A. Knopf, 2011). The first six chapters cover the era of the Psalms.

CHAPTER TWO

"You That Stand in the House of the LORD"

The World of the Psalmists

Since the Psalter reached its present form more than two thousand years ago, it can be no surprise that it reflects a culture significantly different from that of modern readers. Every language is embedded in culture. Language has the astonishing capacity of allowing us to contemplate and criticize our culture and even call for change in it, yet it is never simply free of cultural context. Probably every language in the world expresses some cultural realities that others have trouble articulating, which implies that every language has its limitations and its blind spots as well.

This gives rise to two issues for us to keep in mind as we read the Psalms in English translation. One is the issue of translation in the narrow sense of transposing a text from one language into another. English will never reproduce ancient Hebrew perfectly. At times, NRSV acknowledges this problem by providing an alternative translation in a footnote, but to mention every problem as it arose would make the translation impossibly long and cumbersome. The other issue is the broader one of cultural presuppositions. The ancient Hebrew text assumes that the reader is already in possession of everyday cultural knowledge of the sort that native speakers never think of explaining to one another and may not even be consciously aware of. In our own world, we become aware of these challenges mostly as we try to explain something to a puzzled stranger for whom English is a second language—or whose English was formed in an English-speaking culture different from our own. On a very basic level, think of cricket vs. baseball.

We have already mentioned one important set of cultural issues—those touching on the temple of Jerusalem and the way it provided the center for collection and use of the Psalms. In this chapter, we look at some broader aspects of the society in which the writers and editors of the Psalms lived. The Psalms have become sacred classics of world literature. To a great extent, that automatically means they will seem mysterious, since they are being read by people so far removed from the place and time in which they were written. Even the writings of Shakespeare and other Elizabethan poets can seem quite strange to modern speakers of English and therefore require a fair amount of explanation—and they are only a few centuries old. The world of the Ancient Near East is correspondingly further from us. And, to make things still more complicated, the oldest of the Psalms were written in a time that must already have begun to seem somewhat strange to the final editors of the Psalter. Cultural change happens even in the most stable societies, which means that we may observe some elements of change within this distant culture as well as noting its fundamental difference from ours.

The Presumed Masculine

One thing that strikes many modern readers of the Psalms is the abundance of masculine third-person pronouns: "he, his, him." There is a kind of presumption of maleness: men are the audience of these poems, the singers of them, their primary human focus of interest. This is even more evident in ancient Hebrew than in English translation, since Hebrew distinguishes gender in plural pronouns as well as singular, in second-person pronouns as well as third—and also in verb forms.

This predominance of masculine gender was not simply an accident of grammar. It expressed a basic cultural assumption about gender roles. Sociologists sometimes speak of a "moral division of labor" in ancient Mediterranean cultures. The adult male represented the public face of his family and carried the responsibility for maintaining the family's honor—that is, its public standing and reputation. It was he, not the woman,

> Predominance of masculine gender was not simply an accident of grammar. It expressed a cultural assumption about gender roles.

who would be found in the city gate, negotiating business, participating in legal disputes, and warding off enemies. He was also the warrior, if necessary, and we have seen that warfare was an important matter, particularly in the era of independent Israelite monarchies. The woman, on the other hand, signified the inward-looking aspect of the family; her chief virtue was "shame"—avoidance of anything that might bring reproach on the family and so tend to lower its social standing. She would tend to avoid strangers and perhaps even remain out of sight when possible.

All the texts in the Hebrew Scriptures seem to have passed through editing processes after the destruction of Jerusalem in 586 BCE. To some extent, they may therefore reflect the mores of the post-Exilic period of Israel's history. As far as one can tell, these were more restrictive of women in public than those of the earlier period. In the stories of the patriarchs and of the monarchical period, we encounter a good many strong women. Some of them, such as Jezebel and Athaliah, are roundly condemned for infringing on the male world. Others, like the prophetess Deborah, seem to be admired. Perhaps the model, even early on, was for powerful women to operate "behind a curtain." Think of Sarah, inside the tent, listening in on Abraham's conversation with the three strangers (Gen 18:1–15)! But there are also examples of bold and direct action, as with Abigail, who became David's second wife, (1 Sam 25) or the wealthy woman of Shunem (2 Kgs 4:8–37). By contrast, in our (admittedly more limited) documentation for post-Exilic culture, we encounter few historical women of public distinction. No doubt they existed. If they did not, their fictional counterparts, Esther and Judith, would not have seemed credible even as entertainment. But one wonders whether the "moral division of labor" was being enforced in more limiting ways and whether this made the Psalms more emphatically male-oriented.

Going on Pilgrimage: Psalms 120–34

For an illustration of this presumption of maleness, we can turn to the Songs of Ascents, the small collection of beautiful and well-loved psalms that we took note of previously as a pre-existing element in the compilation of the Psalter. There are reasons to think that these were created in the post-Exilic period and served as prayers for people on their way to Jerusalem for the great annual feasts: Passover in the spring, Shavuoth in the early summer, Succoth in the autumn. They form an interesting context to see how gender roles play out in the Psalms.

Psalm 120 begins with an expression of anxiety about slanderous and hostile neighbors. As the first element in a pilgrimage sequence, it forms an appeal to God to protect the home that, in the pilgrim's absence, may be left as prey to untrustworthy people. While there is nothing in the first few poems of this series that could not have been recited equally well by a woman, it was the absence of the male that would normally be thought of as creating this danger. For that matter, women would have been less likely than men to go on pilgrimage alone.

Living "as an alien in Meshech" or "among the tents of Kedar" may refer to literal exile, for even after the return to Jerusalem increasing numbers of Jewish people were scattered about the Near East and the Mediterranean world in what is called "the Diaspora." Meshech was probably in Asia Minor; Kedar was in the Arabian desert. Together they summed up the sadness of being far from Jerusalem. Even for those who lived closer to Zion, these two distant places are metaphors for unsympathetic neighbors and kinfolk who *act* as if they were foreigners and are prepared to plunder the estate of the departing pilgrim. Either way, a prolonged absence was occasion for anxiety, which comes through clearly in the pilgrim's final declaration:

"Diaspora": the communities of Jews living outside the Land of Israel.

> I am for peace;
>> but when I speak,
>> they are for war. (120:7)

Having thus looked back and prayed for God's protection on the home that is being left behind, the pilgrim is ready to look forward in the words of **Psalm 121**: "I will lift up my eyes to the hills"—that is, to take the road that leads upward to Jerusalem. "Going up" is a literal description of any approach to the city, but it is also a metaphor for return from exile. Wherever the pilgrim is living, to go to Zion is in some sense to go home. At verse 3, the psalm changes speaker. Others now bestow a blessing on the pilgrim, declaring that God will indeed protect this person who is fulfilling the duty of a faithful Israelite. The Hebrew second-person pronouns are masculine here, but could have been heard as implying an indeterminate gender:

> *"Going up" is a literal description of any approach to Jerusalem, but it is also a metaphor for return from exile. Wherever the pilgrim is living, to go to Zion is in some sense to go home.*

> The LORD is your keeper;
>   the LORD is your shade at your right hand.
> The sun shall not strike you by day,
>   nor the moon by night. (121:5–6)

(The danger of sunstroke on such a trek is obvious. The danger of the moon less so, but it was thought capable of its own kind of dangerous influence. Remember that the English word "lunacy" derives from the Latin *luna*, "moon.")

In **Psalm 122**, the pilgrim has reached the goal: "Our feet are standing within your gates, O Jerusalem." The city is the goal because it contains "the house of the LORD," but also because it represents the unity of the nation. The description of the city here emphasizes elements connected with male roles:

> To it the tribes go up,
>   the tribes of the LORD,
> as was decreed for Israel,
>   to give thanks to the name of the LORD.
> For there the thrones of judgment were set up,
>   the thrones of the house of David. (122:4–5)

Tribal membership was inherited through the father; the pilgrimage feasts were a duty for males, though women also attended them; the business of judgment was, as we noted, a male concern, as were the city's walls and towers, on which the pilgrim invokes blessings. This does not, however, narrow the scope of the prayer "Peace be within you"—a prayer for prosperity, justice, and well-being that benefits all alike.

Psalm 123 moves into the temple itself, where Isaiah (6:1) saw the One who is enthroned in majesty. In one of the rare occasions when women are at least implicitly included among the speakers, the psalmist offers a double simile:

> As the eyes of servants
>   look to the hand of their master,
> as the eyes of a maid
>   to the hand of her mistress,
> so our eyes look to the LORD our God,
>   until he has mercy upon us. (123:2)

The following lament about enduring "the scorn of those who are at ease" and "the contempt of the proud" bespeaks the condition of a people who find themselves downtrodden, exposed to grave political and social disadvantage in the places where they live.

Psalm 124 continues this theme of defeat and exile, giving thanks that the people have survived to return yet again on pilgrimage. The vivid imagery of enemies who "would have swallowed us up alive" and who swept over the people like a flash flood prepares us to feel all the more intensely the exhilaration expressed in:

> We have escaped like a bird
>   from the snare of the fowlers;
> the snare is broken
>   and we have escaped. (124:7)

What Psalm 124 recounts as past event, **Psalm 125** recasts as a promise for the future. The God who has rescued Israel from the fowlers will protect the people through whatever comes:

> Those who trust in the LORD are like Mount Zion,
>   which cannot be moved, but abides forever. (125:1)

This is not only an expression of hope in God, but also a reminder to the pilgrims that God will judge those who do wrong, including Israelites. Indeed, the psalmist identifies one of the great dangers of oppression as its tendency to make even the oppressed "stretch out their hands to do wrong." The concluding prayer "Peace be upon Israel" is not only a prayer for national well-being, but for just and righteous conduct. Peace (Hebrew *shalom*) is a way of life, not simply an absence of war.

> "Peace be upon Israel" is not only a prayer for national well-being, but for just and righteous conduct. Peace (Hebrew shalom) is a way of life, not simply an absence of war.

Psalm 126 is one of those psalms whose particular beauty seems to leap over the cultural distance of the centuries and to speak almost as directly now as when it was written. Even a modern urban audience can respond to the agrarian metaphor of its closing prayer:

> May those who sow in tears
> reap with shouts of joy.
> Those who go out weeping,
> bearing the seed for sowing,
> shall come home with shouts of joy,
> carrying their sheaves. (126:5–6)

The metaphor of dream in the opening words that celebrate the restored community in Jerusalem is equally effective:

> When the LORD restored the fortunes of Zion,
> we were like those who dream.
> Then our mouth was filled with laughter,
> and our tongue with shouts of joy. (126:1–2)

This whole series of pilgrimage songs has brought us closer and closer to the goal of the journey. And the reader of the NRSV translation may well have forgotten that the primary focus here is on the *male* pilgrim. Little that is said up to this point in these psalms would have been absolutely exclusive to men, even at the time of writing. And current translation practice has tended to replace the masculine third-person singular pronouns with non-gendered plurals. Thus NRSV concludes Psalm 126 by speaking of "Those who go out weeping" in contrast to the more word-for-word translation of the King James Version: "He that goeth forth and weepeth." The next two psalms in the series, however, make the presumed maleness of the pilgrim fully explicit.

Psalm 127 begins with another vivid reassertion of God's care for Jerusalem and for the people of Israel:

Unless the LORD builds the house,
    those who build it labor in vain,
Unless the LORD guards the city,
    the guard keeps watch in vain.
It is in vain that you rise up early
    and go late to rest,
eating the bread of anxious toil;
    for he gives sleep to his beloved. (127:1–2)

This advice to let anxiety give place to a calm and hopeful spirit through trust in God is applicable to any person of faith—and often needed. It is with some surprise then that the modern reader finds in what follows that the poet has specifically the *male* believer in mind. When we read that "Sons are indeed a heritage from the Lord, the fruit of the womb a reward," we might assume that this applies equally to both father and mother—though we would be more likely to say "children" rather than just "sons." But the psalmist has only the father in view:

Like arrows in the hand of a warrior
    are the sons of one's youth.
Happy is the man who has
    his quiver full of them.
He shall not be put to shame
    when he speaks with his enemies in the gate. (127:4–5)

To have many sons is a promise of the family's continuation, which means fulfillment of the man's moral responsibility in the world and a guarantee of the family's honor.

Psalm 128 also focuses on the male head of household, envisioned as happily ensconced on his farm, supported by his faithful wife and surrounded by his children. The NRSV translation makes this a little confusing by beginning the psalm with the words "Happy is everyone who fears the Lord." The Hebrew actually indicates even in its opening words that this God-fearing person is presumed to be male, which makes the strongly gendered description of human happiness that follows less of a surprise. Still, this remains strange to the modern Western reader, for whom women and men are social and legal equals and morally and spiritually equivalent to one another. A poet in our culture simply cannot address the average person of faith as male. (For that matter, the statistically average Christian is female.) Instead, we have in this ancient text the worshipper as a man who enjoys a productive existence in a flourishing family with a wife who is "like a fruitful vine within your house," where she normally remains.

If such a psalm remains usable in our world, it is at least partly because we tend to "translate" its cultural presuppositions pretty readily into our own changed circumstances. We may be able to identify with its picture of domestic delight without focusing on its precise terms, much as one can recognize a visual representation of family unity even when it depicts a world very different from ours—anything from a Roman fresco to a medieval court scene to a nineteenth-century French painting of a peasant family eating dinner. And, since most psalms do not express the presumption of maleness as bluntly as these two, modern readers find it relatively easy to equate the ancient and the modern god-fearer, regardless of changed assumptions about gender.

> For the modern Western reader, women and men are social and legal equals and morally and spiritually equivalent to one another. A poet in our culture cannot address the average person of faith in terms that presume maleness.

The remaining Songs of Ascents we will treat more briefly here, returning to some of them in later chapters. Here it is enough to point out that **Psalm 129** is constructed around a theme of warfare, including torture inflicted on the losing side. A prayer that curses the oppressors to wither like grass concludes it. It is once again a predominantly male image. Yet, **Psalm 130** is not strongly gendered, and **Psalm 131** even builds around an image of children and mothers. **Psalm 132** tells a political and religious story about how Jerusalem became the heart of Israel—again a concern allotted to males in that culture.

Psalm 133 continues the motif of political peace and prosperity. It is worth spending a few words on this psalm because its key image represents another cultural difference from our world. While perfumes today are generally made with a base of alcohol, in antiquity oil was used for the purpose and guests at a feast were often anointed with perfumed oils. In this case, the oil may be that with which a man from the House of Aaron was consecrated as a priest, but anointing was familiar in many contexts. It appears in Psalm 23, for example, in the context of a banquet. For the modern reader, the following image of a refreshing dewfall in a dry environment may have more direct appeal. With the Psalms, as with all ancient texts, we find ourselves constantly balancing the familiar with the unfamiliar.

Finally, **Psalm 134**, the last of the Songs of Ascents, draws our attention into the temple where we see the faithful spending the night in worship. Our pilgrim, male or female, has indeed reached the goal. And from this position, at the very heart of God's bond with Israel, we receive a benediction:

> May the LORD, maker of heaven and earth,
>> bless you from Zion. (134:3)

The Moral Agent: Psalm 1

In the modern West, both women and men function as public persons. The contrast with ancient practice creates a challenge for translators, and nowhere is the challenge greater than in the Psalms. As we have noted, most of the scriptures (and most literature in general) speaks *to* the reader. The Psalms, most of the time, speak *for* the reader. One can read them, of course, without accepting them as one's own voice. But Christians have also chosen, for many centuries, to take them as voicing our relationship with God. When we do so, we have to make some judgments about linguistic equivalents.

Think, for example, of **Psalm 1**. Older translations begin the poem with a specifically masculine reference:

> Blessed is the man that walketh not in the counsel of the
> ungodly. (1:1 KJV)

But what was the point of this benediction—that only righteous men are blessed and not righteous women? Hardly! The point is that every person who behaves righteously in public transactions is blessed. A word-for-word translation of the Hebrew, then, can actually be misleading in modern English. This is why the NRSV translators have shifted to plural pronouns that, in English, avoid the question of gender.

> Happy are those
> who do not follow the advice of the wicked,

or take the path that sinners tread,
   or sit in the seat of scoffers;
but their delight is in the law of the LORD,
   and on his law they meditate day and night. (1:1–2)

The message of the poem is that virtue and faithfulness are linked to the true flourishing of human life:

They are like trees
   planted by streams of water,
which yield their fruit in its season,
   and their leaves do not wither.
In all that they do, they prosper. (1:3)

This could serve as a portrait of the ideal worshipper in the temple—probably the reason why the editors placed it at the beginning of the Psalter. The wicked, by contrast, are doomed to judgment and defeat. To sing God's praises requires not mere attendance on religious services, but commitment to a life of integrity. Of course, one can ask how well the psalm's optimistic connection between virtue and success holds up in actual human life, but not every psalm can deal with every aspect of human experience. As we shall see, there are plenty of psalms that tell the other side of the story—the reality of innocent suffering.

> What was the point of the benediction in Psalm 1—that only men who are righteous are blessed and not women? Hardly! The point is that every person who behaves righteously in public transactions is blessed.

The King: Psalm 89

The congregation of the temple was, ideally, co-extensive with the adult male population of Israelites, even though they could never all be assembled there at the same time. Since this was also the citizen body of the nation, it was normal that the interests and concerns of the community would intertwine with those of the sanctuary. In the period of the First Temple (the tenth to the early sixth centuries BCE), this meant a prominent role for the king. At first, David and Solomon ruled over the whole nation of Israel. After Solomon, the kingdom split in two, with the ten northern tribes retaining the name "Israel" while the southern kingdom, with Jerusalem as its capital

The congregation of the temple was also the citizen body of the nation. Accordingly, the interests and concerns of the community intertwined with those of the sanctuary. In the period of the First Temple, this meant a prominent role for the king.

and sanctuary, took the name of "Judah." But the king of Israel had a royal temple, too—located at Bethel—and must have had somewhat the same relation to it as the king of Judah had to the Jerusalem temple. Indeed, we see this linkage in action when the priest of Bethel warned Amos off by telling him that this was a royal sanctuary (Amos 7:10–12). It is possible, then, that we have some psalms from the northern sanctuary along with those from Jerusalem in the Psalter, though it is difficult to identify them with complete confidence.

The king was not a "secular" figure in the modern sense. Kingship was as much a sacred role as priesthood. The king was God's "Anointed," a title also represented in English by the terms "Messiah," derived from Hebrew, and "Christ," derived from Greek. **Psalm 89** shows how sacred and political elements merged in the person of the king of Judah. The central part of it seems to echo some of the enthronement ritual for a new monarch or for the anniversary of such an event. It speaks to God:

> Then you spoke in a vision to your faithful one, and said:
>   "I have set the crown on one who is mighty,
>   I have exalted one chosen from the people.
> I have found my servant David;
>   with my holy oil I have anointed him;
> my hand shall always remain with him;
>   my arm also shall strengthen him." (89:19–21)

The reference here to "David" could also refer to any of his descendants in the dynasty that ruled Judah.

To the king, God promises victory in war, empire (one hand on the Mediterranean Sea and one on the rivers of modern Iraq, v. 25), and an intimate relationship with God:

> "He shall cry to me, 'You are my Father,
>   my God, and the Rock of my salvation!'
> I will make him the firstborn,
>   the highest of the kings of the earth.

> Forever will I keep my steadfast love for him,
>   and my covenant with him will stand firm. (89:26–28)

God will punish David's descendants if they do not adhere to God's commandments, but God promises never to let David's royal line fail:

> "Once and for all I have sworn by my holiness;
>   I will not lie to David.
> His line shall continue forever,
>   and his throne endure before me like the sun." (89:35–36)

This royal ideology includes a strong element of martial prowess. (For two other fine examples, read Psalms 20 and 21; Psalms 60 and 61 are also of interest.) War was an inescapable reality of the period. Judah and Israel were two small kingdoms among others of similar power: Moab, Edom and Ammon (all in modern Jordan) and Aram (centered on Damascus). They fought one another for territory and plunder. They built fortified cities for defense. They built up armies that included expensive chariots and horses. This is not to say that they were always eager to go to war with one another; but they were constantly on alert against attack. To some extent, each kingdom could advance its own fortunes only by taking something from its neighbors.

War was an inescapable reality of the period.

In addition, the much greater power of Egypt was an intermittent threat to all these small states, and Assyria and Babylonia eventually laid waste to both Israel and Judah. Maintaining peace was one royal goal, but it was difficult to imagine how it would come about except through the defeat of enemies. And, of course, peace was at odds with another goal: the aggrandizement of the king's country and capital and the accompanying increase in the king's honor.

The kingship of David, in this psalm, is a reflection of the kingship of God, described earlier on:

> You rule the raging of the sea;
>   when its waves rise, you still them.
> You crushed Rahab [a mythical sea monster] like a carcass;
>   you scattered your enemies with your mighty arm. (89:9–10)

Righteousness and justice were essential foundations of kingship.

God's power, however, is not arbitrary. Just as the king is bound to "walk according to [God's] ordinances" (v. 30), God's own throne is founded on the ethics of true kingship:

> Righteousness and justice are the foundation of your throne;
>> steadfast love and faithfulness go before you. (89:14)

This royal ethic of just power is the reason the faithful king can dare to address God as "my Father, my God, and the Rock of my salvation."

The central section of Psalm 89 (roughly verses 5–37) represents the kind of royal ideology that had developed over the centuries of Israelite independence. As it stands, however, it is embraced by materials that speak, explicitly or implicitly, of a national life when the king is either powerless or non-existent:

> But now you have spurned and rejected him;
>> you are full of wrath against your anointed. (89:38)

> You have removed the scepter from his hand,
>> and hurled his throne to the ground.
> You have cut short the days of his youth;
>> you have covered him with shame. (89:44–45)

Even the opening of the psalm, with its insistence on God's faithfulness, seems to point forward to the disaster, as if it "protested too much":

> I will sing of your steadfast love, O LORD, forever;
>> with my mouth I will proclaim your faithfulness to all
>>> generations.
> I declare that your steadfast love is established forever;
>> your faithfulness is as firm as the heavens. (89:1–2)

The psalmist's initial declaration of faith lays the groundwork for the accusation to follow—that God has not, in fact, given what God promised.

This kind of bold confrontation with God is not at all rare in the Psalms. Our poets' understanding of prayer allows for or even requires a high standard of honesty in expression. Another good example is Psalm 44, where the poet concludes by saying, rather rudely:

Rouse yourself! Why do you sleep, O Lord?
  Awake, do not cast us off forever! (44:23)

The final section of Psalm 89 is an appeal for God to restore the kingship. Verse 47 can be read as an utterance by an existing king who is at the end of his rope; this seems to be the understanding of the NRSV translators. But the Hebrew, as they observe in the footnote, is unclear. And it seems more probable, on the whole, that the existing form of the psalm was created after the destruction of the kingdom and intends rather to appeal for a *restoration* of the Davidic house. Thus it illustrates not only the basic ideology of kingship, but its continuing power even long after it disappeared. (The perplexing benediction in the psalm's final verse, as we noted above, is the closing benediction for Book III of the Psalter, added by the final editors, and not an integral part of the psalm itself.)

Royal Marriage: Psalms 45, 93

War, of course, was not the only instrument of royal power. Marriage was another, whether it served to connect the king with powerful families within the nation or to cement foreign alliances. In a world that took multiple wives as a given for powerful men, such marriages perhaps ranked less prominently in the public eye than the making of war, but we do find one royal marriage commemorated in **Psalm 45**, a poem that celebrates both bride and groom. To the king, the psalmist writes:

You are the most handsome of men:
  grace is poured upon your lips:
  therefore God has blessed you forever. (45:2)

The king is also, of course, a warrior and is exhorted to gain victory. To the bride, the poet offers a description of her own anticipated appearance with her attendants:

The princess is decked in her chamber with gold-woven robes;
  in many-colored robes she is led to the king;
  behind her the virgins, her companions, follow. (45:13–14)

But there are other dimensions, too, to the marriage, which is apparently part of an alliance with Tyre:

Hear, O daughter, consider and incline your ear;
  forget your people and your father's house,
  and the king will desire your beauty.
Since he is your lord, bow to him;
  the people of Tyre will seek your favor with gifts,
  the richest of people with all kinds of wealth. (45:10–13)

In the center of the poem stands praise for the king's justice and righteousness (45:6–7), which was as central to the understanding of kingship as martial prowess. It also contains some language that seems to exalt the king even further than we would have expected:

Your throne, O God, endures forever and ever. (45:6)

NRSV provides an alternative translation in the footnote in an effort to avoid the suggestion that the king could actually be addressed as "god." But there can be no doubt that the royal office on earth was seen both as parallel to that of God and as intimately linked to it.

Marriage served to connect the king with powerful families within the nation or to cement foreign alliances.

Psalm 93 reverses the process by celebrating God in royal terms: "The LORD is king, he is robed in majesty." To be sure, God's kingship is not exactly like that of a mortal. God wins the right to rule through creation rather than conquest:

He has established the world; it shall never be moved;
  your throne is established from of old;
  you are from everlasting. (93:1c-2)

But even here, there is a hint of struggle and victory. Drawing on old Canaanite mythology, the poet hints that God created through triumphing over the primeval waters, the powers of chaos:

The floods have lifted up, O LORD,
  the floods have lifted up their voice;
  the floods lift up their roaring.
More majestic than the thunders of mighty waters,
  more majestic than the waves of the sea,
  majestic on high is the LORD! (93:3–4)

Justice and Peace: Psalm 72

Psalm 72 is another royal psalm, similar to the ones we have just looked at in that it appeals to God to give power to the king, but this time the power requested is not for war, but for justice and righteousness:

> May he judge your people with righteousness,
>   and your poor with justice. (72:2)

The king as warrior was a necessity of the times, but the king as just judge remained central to Israelite understanding of the office. It is not surprising to find this psalm attributed to Solomon, who was said to have chosen the gift of a wise and discerning heart over long life, riches, or the lives of his enemies (1 Kgs 3:3–14).

Justice is itself part of a larger ideal of peace, the Hebrew "shalom," which embraces the well-being of the natural world as well, bestowing not only absence of conflict but general well-being.

Justice is itself part of a larger ideal of peace, the Hebrew "shalom," which embraces the well-being of the natural world as well, bestowing not only absence of conflict but general well-being:

> May the mountains yield prosperity for the people,
>   and the hills, in righteousness. (72:3)

The king's reign will be a kind of return to paradise:

> May he be like rain that falls on the mown grass,
>   like showers that water the earth.
> In his days may righteousness flourish
>   and peace abound, until the moon is no more. (72:6–7)

The well-being of the people and that of the land depend on each other.

The psalm continues by asking for sweeping dominion and the defeat of all enemies. Even the far off kings of Tarshish (in modern Spain) will bring tribute. But the reason given for this is that

> . . . [the king] delivers the needy when they call,
>   the poor and those who have no helper.
> He has pity on the weak and the needy,
>   and saves the lives of the needy.

> From oppression and violence he redeems their life;
>   and precious is their blood in his sight. (72:12–14)

The psalm forms a fitting conclusion, as the final verse says, to "the prayers of David son of Jesse," providing as it does a compelling description of the perfect king.

The picture of the king given here, in fact, is so idealized that one might imagine that it really speaks not of any historical monarch, but of the longed-for future Anointed One, the Messiah, and Christians have certainly read it as such. But, as we noted, kingship was a sacred office in ancient Israel and Judah. Individual monarchs may have failed to live up to expectation. (Has there been any era of human history when this was not sometimes true of community leaders?) But this psalm represented the ever-renewed hope for the kingship, framed in terms of the centrality of justice in the civic ideals of ancient Israel.

Psalm 72 was the inspiration for James Montgomery's hymn "Hail to the Lord's Anointed."

The Community of the Second Temple: Psalm 115

The world of the Second Temple was different from the first. Jerusalem was no longer capital of an independent kingdom. Its destruction by the Babylonians left only ruins and, with much of the leadership carried off into exile in what is now Iraq, only a small remnant was left to worship as best it could on Mount Zion. But fifty years later, after the Persians conquered Babylon and the emperor Cyrus gave Jewish exiles permission to return, a slow and often difficult process of rebuilding began.

Protracted though the process was, the prolonged period of relative peace under Persian rule gave time for the impoverished community to bring the temple back to some of its former prestige and beauty. Like other ancient temples, it became once again a center of wealth both because people made offerings to it and also because it served as a safe place where people could deposit funds and expect to reclaim them later.

There was no king of Judah during this period. There was a governor, appointed by the Persian king, who was himself at least sometimes Jewish. But the high priest of the temple assumed particular prominence as local leader of the community. This is the period when the Hebrew Scriptures, including the Psalter, began to be collected, edited, and revised. There was a desire to guard the earlier tradition—evident, for example, in the many royal psalms that survive in the collection. They had no immediate use in terms of royal ceremonies, but they expressed the faith of ancient Israel and held out the hope of a future kingdom that would fulfill God's promise to David.

At the same time, the faith of Israel could not simply focus on a royal past or even a hoped-for royal future. It was important to celebrate the community's existing life under priestly leadership. Hence, as we saw in Chapter 1, Psalm 135 summed up the Temple's congregation as comprised of the house of Israel, the house of Aaron, and the house of Levi. The priestly tribe (Levi) and the high priestly family (Aaron) fulfill the role of public leadership here. The same point is made in **Psalm 115**, which twice sums up the congregation as consisting of the house of Israel, the house of Aaron, and the house of Levi (vv. 9–13).

Persian rule gave this community time to grow and consolidate itself. But in the late fourth century BCE, Alexander of Macedon destroyed the Persian Empire and inaugurated several centuries of Greek dominion. At his early death, his principal generals divided the new empire among themselves, and Judah fell initially to the share of Ptolemy, whose capital was Alexandria in Egypt.

Under Ptolemaic rule, Judah experienced a continuation of the stability the Persians had brought. The Ptolemies took a significant interest in their Jewish subjects and may well have had a hand in organizing the Greek translation of the Torah, which became known as the Septuagint. It was in this Greek form that many Jews in the Mediterranean Diaspora henceforth knew the Torah. The Ptolemies' interest in the Torah was natural enough, since it formed the legal corpus of a major subject people in their empire. But the Jewish community itself took the process of translating much further. The Psalter, too, was included, and this collection of translations formed the first Old Testament of Christians.

Interestingly, there are some differences between the Greek and Hebrew Psalters, suggesting that the Hebrew manuscripts used for the translation may have varied in some respects from those on which the authoritative Hebrew text came to be based. The most obvious difference is that the numbering of most of the Psalms in Greek differs slightly from that in Hebrew. Thus, for example, the long psalm numbered 119 in Hebrew and in most English translations, is Psalm 118 in Greek. (The numbering never varies by more than one digit.)

We can get a sense of the splendor and authority of a high priest in this era from a book of the Apocrypha variously called "Ecclesiasticus" or "The Wisdom of Jesus Son of Sirach" or simply "Sirach." The passage describes the high priest Simon, son of Onias, a distinguished leader and a great builder, who enhanced both the temple itself and the city as a whole. His public appearances in worship were splendid in every way:

> How glorious he was, surrounded by the people,
>   as he came out of the house of the curtain.
> Like the morning star among the clouds,
>   like the full moon at the festal season;
> like the sun shining on the temple of the Most High,
>   like the rainbow gleaming in splendid clouds;
> like roses in the days of first fruits,
>   like lilies by a spring of water,
>   like a green shoot on Lebanon on a summer day...
>   (Sirach 50:5–8)

Such a figure clearly combined elements of kingship with those of priesthood and functioned as the central representative figure for the Jewish population in and around Jerusalem—and indeed for Jews much further afield.

But Simon came at the end of the era of peace. Jerusalem was caught up in rivalries between the Ptolemies and the rival Seleucid family, whose capital lay to the north, in Antioch, on the coast of modern Turkey. Not far behind the Seleucids loomed the power of Rome. All in all, the period from about 190 BCE to the late first century BCE was filled with civil conflict and danger. The collision of empires made possible a century of Jewish independence under a priestly dynasty that made themselves kings as well until the Romans pushed them aside in 63 BCE. The temple survived these troubles and was rebuilt on a grand scale at the initiative of a very unlikely individual, Herod the Great. Son of an Edomite convert to Judaism, he was made king of the Jews (among other titles) by the Romans. During his long reign (and continuing over some decades afterward), the temple reached its greatest peak of splendor, only to be destroyed by the Roman general Titus when he captured Jerusalem during the First Jewish War of 66–70 CE.

Through all this, many basic presuppositions of everyday life in the area around Jerusalem may not have changed a great deal. Family structure was still dominated by the presumption of masculinity and the moral division of labor we mentioned earlier. The country around Jerusalem was still divided up among many different ethnic groups, now with the addition of large numbers of Greek-speaking people, some of them Jews, some Gentiles. The attraction of Greek culture, dominant throughout the Near East at this point, sometimes created problems for Jews. But the Psalter, now in two languages, continued to be a central element in the life and faith of Jewish people.

Continuing the Conversation:

Some translators have endeavored to take a step beyond NRSV in eliminating gender-specific terms not only for human beings, but for God. Two examples:

The New Testament and Psalms: An Inclusive Version (New York: Oxford University Press, 1995)

The St. Helena Psalter (New York: Church Publishing, 2004)

Any reader who would like access to the ancient Greek version of the Psalms will find help in *A Comparative Psalter*, ed. John R. Kohlenberger III (New York: Oxford University Press, 2007). It contains parallel Hebrew and Greek texts with translation of each.

CHAPTER THREE

"O Sing to the LORD a New Song"

Hymns of Praise and Songs of Worship

How Ancient Hebrew Poetry Worked: Psalm 23

One psalm can seem quite different from the next as we read our way through the Psalter, but most of them, in fact, can be grouped into a few "genres" (basic types) of poetry, the most common being hymns, laments, and thanksgivings. In this chapter, we look particularly at the first type, the hymn, which expresses awe, wonder, and praise. We have already encountered several of these—for example, Psalms 29 and 150—but have not thought specifically in terms of what form they take.

The most common genres of poetry in the Psalter are hymns, laments, and thanksgivings.

The Psalms exemplify not only the genres, but also the "prosody" of ancient Hebrew poetry—the way it constructed poetic lines. It differed from the traditional modes of English poetry, which tend to use fixed rhythmic patterns organized by combinations of stressed and unstressed syllables. Take, for example, the opening lines of a well-loved hymn based on **Psalm 23**:

> The Kíng of lóve my shépherd ís,
>   whose goódness faíleth néver . . .

The rhythm of ancient Hebrew poetry comes through pretty clearly in English translation, since English, like Hebrew, tends to have short words and strong stress accents.

This same pattern of accented and unaccented syllables (called "meter") is repeated over and over throughout the hymn. There are many possible meters, and each follows its own distinctive pattern.

Ancient Hebrew poetry, in comparison, was less concerned about the exact number of syllables, but it was attentive to the overall number of stresses (or accents) in each line. The most common pattern was to arrange poetic lines in couplets and give each line a limited number of major stresses—three was most common, but two and four were also possible. This structure comes through pretty clearly in English translation, since English, like Hebrew, tends to have short words and strong stress accents. The match between the two languages is not perfect, of course, but it is close enough to illustrate the process.

Here, for example, is the beginning of Psalm 23, in NRSV, and the accent marks indicate roughly where the stresses fall in the Hebrew original:

> The LÓRD is my shépherd, I shall not wánt.
> > He makes me líe down in greén pástures;
> he leáds me beside stíll wáters;
> > he restóres my soúl. (23:1–3)

This gives us three three-stress lines followed by one two-stress line. If I were marking the stresses here strictly in terms of the English language, they would be a little different:

> The LÓRD is my shépherd, I sháll not wánt.
> > He mákes me lie dówn in green pástures;
> he leáds me besíde still wáters;
> > he restóres my soúl.

Still, there is a broad equivalence between the two. The only major difference is that our first line now has four accented syllables.

This means that if we read the psalms aloud in translation, we can actually get some notion of the Hebrew prosody behind them. This has helped make the psalms relatively easy to translate into other languages, and no doubt this has helped secure their popularity among

Christians, who could work out ways to sing them in Greek, Latin, and other languages without too much difficulty.

Ancient Hebrew poetry, like that of other languages, also uses simile, metaphor, unusual or unexpected vocabulary, and a whole range of other verbal devices. One particular aspect of it, however, is worth noting here—and has also contributed to ease of translation. Hebrew poetry did not use verbal rhyme as a structural element, but it did use a kind of "rhyming" of thoughts or phrases, referred to as "parallelism." In each couplet, the second line typically parallels the first somehow. It may use a similar grammatical construction or it may reiterate the same thought in a different way.

> Hebrew poetry did not use verbal rhyme as a structural element, but it did use a kind of rhyming of thoughts referred to as "parallelism."

Thus, in Psalm 23, the first line declares, in general terms, that God's care for me leaves me free from want; the second line phrases that same thought more concretely (and more in terms of the sheep's perspective) as resting in green pastures. The second couplet works in much the same way: God gives access to water which is then paralleled with reviving our soul, i.e., our energy and vitality. Parallelism ties each couplet together, and the couplets are woven together into a vivid and concrete image of God as shepherd tending to the needs of the flock.

There are yet other ways to construct the parallelism. Sometimes, the two lines are virtual opposites—danger, for example, countered by fearlessness:

> Even though I walk through the darkest valley,
>   I fear no evil. (23:4)

In other cases, the second line of the couplet simply continues the thought without any obvious parallelism, as in

> He leads me in right paths
>   for his name's sake. (23:3)

Yet, this couplet, as a whole, serves as a kind of parallel to the first line of Psalm 23: "The Lord is my shepherd, I shall not want." God will lead us along the right paths *because* he is shepherd. Meanwhile, the two intervening lines, about green pastures and still waters, are effectively parallel to each other. This makes a kind of ABBA pattern in the first two couplets, with the third couplet paralleling and thus reinforcing the first and fourth lines (the "A" parallels).

> The LORD is my shepherd, I shall not want.
> . . .
>> he restores my soul
> . . .
> He leads me in right paths
>> for his name's sake.

Obviously, parallelism was a very flexible and versatile tool for the ancient Hebrew poet. Noticing the subtle ways in which our poets work with the device can add to our understanding of the Psalms and our enjoyment of them.

Hymns: Psalms 96, 97, 117

Parallelism pervades all the psalms. The distinct genres, on the other hand, functioned as patterns for constructing particular types of psalms. Of these genres, the hymn is the simplest and most immediately obvious. This does not mean that the hymns themselves are simple; only that the basic patterns are. The exuberant imagination that the poets brought to their work makes each distinctive.

The basic formula for a hymn is simply a summons to praise God followed by a list of reasons.

The basic formula for a hymn is simply a summons to praise God followed by a list of reasons. Sometimes the reasons take the form of a narrative. Sometimes they are attached as clauses beginning with "for": "O come, let us sing to the LORD. . . . For the LORD is a great God, and a great King above all gods" (95:1, 3). At still other times, they are attached with a relative pronoun ("who"):

> Bless the LORD, O my soul.
>> O LORD my God, thou art very great;
>> thou art clothed with honour and majesty.
> Who coverest thyself with light as with a garment:
>> who stretchest out the heavens like a curtain. (104:1–2, KJV)

(This use of relative pronouns is not always possible to detect in NRSV, which tends to break up long sentences and turn "who" into a personal pronoun: "*You* are ... wrapped in light as with a garment. *You* stretch out the heavens like a tent. ...")

Psalm 117, the shortest of all the psalms, manages to create a complete hymn in just two verses. First, the exhortation to praise:

> Praise the LORD, all you nations!
>   Extol him, all you peoples! (117:1)

Then the reason, followed by a *hallelujah* that reiterates the call to praise:

> For great is his steadfast love toward us,
>   and the faithfulness of the LORD endures forever.
> Praise the LORD! (117:2)

Compact as it is, it still has all the energy and liveliness of a good hymn.

Psalm 96 is a more typical example of the genre. It begins with the exhortation: "O sing to the LORD a new song." The word "new" must have been a literal description of the psalm when it was first performed, but, ancient as it now is, it still implies that there is no end to the making of hymns—and that praise is renewed with each singing. The poet then goes on to establish the broadest possible scope for praise: "sing to the LORD, all the earth."

The God worshipped in the temple at Jerusalem was indeed the God of Israel, but equally the creator of the whole world and of all the people in it. The psalmist begins with Israel, exhorting the congregation to "tell of his salvation from day to day." Presumably the salvation in question is primarily the saving acts God has done on behalf of Israel. Israel, in turn, can proclaim them to others:

> Declare his glory among the nations,
>   his marvelous works among all the peoples. (96:3)

After all, "the gods of the peoples are idols, but the LORD made the heavens." Since God is universal, even Gentiles ought to be turning toward Jerusalem, where "strength and beauty are in his sanctuary," to sing hymns of praise.

Verses 7–9 elaborate on this theme, presenting us with a picture of all the families of the earth converging on the temple with offerings and praise. There is good reason for all humanity to rejoice:

> Say among the nations, "The LORD is king!
>> The world is firmly established; it shall never be moved.
>> He will judge the peoples with equity." (96:10)

God's reign is one of truth and justice and will prevail over falsehood and oppression to the advantage of all humankind.

But then the psalm broadens out into a still more universal perspective. If God is indeed the maker of the world (v. 5), then the whole universe can appropriately join in the celebration, for God is as directly and intimately linked to the physical world as to that of human beings:

> Let the heavens be glad, and let the earth rejoice;
>> let the sea roar, and all that fills it;
>> let the field exult, and everything in it.
> Then shall all the trees of the forest sing for joy
>> before the LORD; for he is coming,
>> for he is coming to judge the earth. (96:11–13)

There is a sense in this passage that the physical world, the "environment" as we have come to call it, can have a certain expectation of divine justice, too. The reign of God, made tangible in God's day of judgment, will vindicate the whole world.

The invitation for the natural world to join in God's praises is not an incidental notion found in only one or two psalms; it is pervasive.

This is not an incidental notion found in only one or two psalms; it is pervasive. **Psalm 97** begins by summoning the world to praise in phrases that could include its human inhabitants but actually specify only the lands themselves:

> The LORD is king! Let the earth rejoice;
>> let the many coastlands be glad! (97:1)

Then it goes on to celebrate a God who is deeply involved in the physical world:

> Clouds and thick darkness are all around him;
>> righteousness and justice are the foundation of his throne.
> Fire goes before him,
>> and consumes his adversaries on every side.

His lightnings light up the world;
    the earth sees and trembles.
The mountains melt like wax before the LORD,
    before the Lord of all the earth. (97:2–5)

God's splendor in the natural world is a worthy topic of praise in itself, but often, as here, it is linked to God's devotion to justice. Near the end of the psalm we read:

The LORD loves those who hate evil;
    he guards the lives of his faithful;
    he rescues them from the hand of the wicked. (97:10)

Then, in an image that ties this back to the nature-imagery at the beginning:

Light dawns for the righteous,
    and joy for the upright in heart. (97:11)

The central part of the psalm includes another motif found in many hymns—the uselessness of idols. Images of divinities were the religious norm in the Ancient Near East, and the absence of such an image became a sign of two seemingly contradictory aspects of Israel's God. On the one hand, God is universal and cannot be portrayed. On the other, God *dwells* in Zion, which therefore can have no place for a representation of One who is always present. Psalm 97 unites these, not with theological reasoning, but with the poetry of joy:

The heavens proclaim his righteousness:
    and all the peoples behold his glory.
All worshippers of images are put to shame,
    those who make their boast in worthless idols:
    all gods bow down before him.
Zion hears and is glad,
    and the towns of Judah rejoice,
    because of your judgments, O God.
For you, O LORD, are most high over all the earth;
    you are exalted far above all gods. (97:6–9)

The existence of other gods, as we have seen before, is not necessarily denied. But they are sharply subordinated to the one truly universal deity. And their images are made a sign, not of their power, but of their inferior status.

For additional examples of the hymn genre, look at Psalms 98, 99, 100 (all relatively brief) and, for longer examples, Psalms 103 and 105.

Flexibility of the Hymn Style:
Psalms 46, 107, 136

Simple as the basic hymn genre was, it gave room for great exercise of poetic ingenuity and imagination. **Psalm 46**, for example, omits the normal summons to praise God and bursts directly into proclamation of the reasons for celebration:

> God is our refuge and strength,
> a very present help in trouble.
> Therefore we will not fear, though the earth should change,
> though the mountains shake in the heart of the sea;
> though its waters roar and foam,
> though the mountains tremble with its tumult. *Selah* (46:1–3)

The threat is described here with the force of ancient mythological images, in which the sea was perceived as a kind of primeval "black hole," the power of chaos threatening to drag the rest of the world into its orbit.

Luther's hymn "A mighty fortress is our God" is based on Psalm 46.

But we have seen from other psalms that God is "enthroned over the flood," compelling the waters to remain within bounds. The poet reminds us dramatically of this by shifting attention directly from the chaotic sea to "the river of God," the heavenly waters that descend on Jerusalem as dew and rain:

> There is a river whose streams make glad the city of God,
> the holy habitation of the Most High. (46:4)

The nations, like the sea, are "in an uproar," but God will help Zion "when the morning dawns." In part, then, this is a celebration of Israelite victory over their enemies: "see what desolations [God] has brought on the earth." But the poet changes it from a vision of present destruction to one of future peace:

He makes wars cease to the end of the earth;
　　he breaks the bow, and shatters the spear;
　　he burns the shields with fire. (46:9)

Then we hear the voice of God addressing us:

"Be still, and know that I am God!
　　I am exalted among the nations,
　　I am exalted in the earth." (46:10)

Even in a collection as rich as the Psalter, Psalm 46 stands out as a particularly brilliant piece of poetry. It is a celebratory expression of praise that is, at the same time, a psalm of thanksgiving for deliverance from enemies and a vision of future peace for the whole world—and it does all this in just eleven verses.

A psalm writer could equally well expand the hymnic form to considerable length. **Psalm 107** does this by presenting a set of hypothetical situations in which people have been in danger, have called on God, and have been delivered. Taken as a whole, the scenarios all appear to be pointing toward the hope of a continuing restoration of Israel through return from exile. It is a complex and carefully wrought poem, bringing together multiple elements in its larger structure. The summons to praise serves to focus its broader concerns:

O give thanks to the LORD, for he is good;
　　for his steadfast love endures forever.
Let the redeemed of the LORD say so,
　　those he redeemed from trouble
and gathered in from the lands,
　　from the east and from the west,
　　from the north and from the south. (107:1–3)

Then follow four episodes of people in life-threatening situations: lost in the desert, imprisoned in dungeons, suffering fatal illness, caught by a storm on the sea. In each case, after they call on God and are delivered, the psalmist exhorts them to offer thanks:

Let them thank the LORD for his steadfast love,
　　for his wonderful works to humankind. (107:8, 15, 21, 31)

To each repetition of this appeal is attached a brief reason specific to the trouble described.

Next, the poet offers two images of God's care for the righteous. One is based in nature: God can turn rivers into deserts (to punish the wicked) and deserts into pools of water (to rescue those in need). The people of the Ancient Near East had had more than one opportunity to see evidence of such ecological shifts, some of them, of course, caused by human destructiveness. The second image is social: God can overthrow oppressors and make them "wander in trackless wastes," while raising up the needy. Finally, the psalm concludes with a kind of "moral," a summing up of its message:

> The upright see it and are glad;
>> and all wickedness stops its mouth.
> Let those who are wise give heed to these things,
>> and consider the steadfast love of the LORD. (107:42–43)

This may seem a bit pat. In fact, we know (and the Psalter as a whole knows) that sometimes the wicked thrive and the righteous suffer. But the psalmist is not entirely wrong, either. Salvation can, in fact, arrive contrary to all expectation.

Another element of diversity in the hymnic psalms may have come in the realm of performance, though that is harder for us to discern. One wonders, for example, why Psalm 46, brief as it is, contains three Selahs, the last of them, quite unusually, at the end. Perhaps the instrumental music carried a particularly large role in establishing its celebratory character. Most of the hymns in the Psalter were probably composed for performance by professional musicians, whose contributions will have brought these texts to life in ways that we can only imagine.

Another element of variation in the hymnic psalms, harder to discern, may have come in the realm of performance, through the number and placement of instrumental interludes and through the interplay of solo voices and antiphonal choruses.

Another element that may suggest something about performance is the frequency with which the voice speaking in a psalm can change. We see this, for example, in Psalm 87, which begins with a description of Zion and an address to the city: "Glorious things are spoken of you." (87:3) But then it shifts unexpectedly into the first person, as if the city itself were speaking:

"Among those who know me I mention Rahab and Babylon." We can guess that such abrupt transitions might have been opportunities for a solo voice or for antiphonal choirs.

There is not much to suggest that the psalms would originally have been sung by the whole congregation. Book technology did not permit mass production of texts. Shorter psalms, such as the Songs of Ascents, could easily have been memorized, but longer ones would require prolonged exposure (or rote teaching) to make that possible. At least one psalm, however, **Psalm 136**, has a kind of call-and-response structure suggesting a musical dialogue. The poem also has a classic hymn structure, beginning with the repeated exhortation to "give thanks to the LORD." In this case, NRSV has preserved the succession of relative clauses: "who alone does great wonders ... , who by understanding made the heavens . . ." and so on. But every second line of the psalm is exactly the same: "for his steadfast love endures forever." It would have been easy for the assembled multitude to pick up such a refrain.

The chorus or solo voice that leads the singing works its way through a wide array of evidences for God's greatness, starting with God's exalted status among the supernatural beings—"God of gods," "Lord of lords." We then hear about God as creator, with echoes of Genesis 1, and there follows a recounting of some high points of God's intervention during the Exodus from Egypt and the wilderness years. There is an emphasis here on martial feats such as the overthrow of Pharaoh's army at the Red Sea (Exod 14) and the deaths of the enemy kings Sihon and Og (Num 21). This could seem narrowly militaristic, but the psalmist reminds the congregation that God did this for the people when they were unable to do it for themselves:

It is he who remembered us in our low estate, . . .
and rescued us from our foes, . . . (136:23–24)

The psalmist concludes by describing God in more universal terms as the one "who gives food to all flesh." Like the texts we have looked at in previous chapters, hymns embrace a diverse array of perspectives on God, not troubling to resolve potential tensions, but claiming all of them as opportunities of celebration.

Liturgies: Psalms 24, 121, 132

Some other psalms that were not strictly hymns in the narrow sense of the term have features similar to those of Psalm 136, suggesting that they, too, were used for liturgical performance in which a chorus or even the whole congregation might join. **Psalm 24**, for example, begins with a hymn-like celebration of God's greatness:

> The earth is the LORD's and all that is in it,
>   the world, and those who live in it;
> for he has founded it on the seas,
>   and established it on the rivers. (24:1–2)

The reference to the seas and rivers here again derives from the the Ancient Near Eastern vision of the earth as a kind of disc, floating on water and covered with the transparent dome of the firmament, with more waters above it.

Some psalms have features suggesting that they were used for liturgical perform-ance, in which a chorus or even the whole congrega-tion might join.

After this introduction, however, the psalm shifts into a call-and-response format that sounds as if it would have been divided between a soloist and a chorus or between two antiphonal choruses. At issue is entrance into the temple, both for the worshippers and for God. The first voice asks:

> Who shall ascend the hill of the LORD?
>   And who shall stand in his holy place? (24:3)

The second voice answers:

> Those who have clean hands and pure hearts,
>   who do not life up their souls to what is false,
>   and do not swear deceitfully. (24:4)

An instrumental interlude follows, and then the second, more complex round of call and response turns its attention toward God, who will meet the worshippers here in the temple. The first voice addresses the gates:

> Lift up your heads, O gates!
>   and be lifted up, O ancient doors!
>   that the King of glory may come in. (24:7)

Then a second voice—the voice, as it were, of the gates themselves—asks, "Who is the King of glory?" The response, probably by the first voice, is:

> The LORD, strong and mighty,
>   the LORD, mighty in battle. (24:8)

This threefold sequence is then repeated before the psalm concludes with another instrumental performance. The overall effect is exhilarating even now and even without its music. It must have been much more so in the temple itself at the beginning of some major pilgrimage festival.

We noted earlier that the Songs of Ascents (Psalms 120–34) were also related to pilgrimage, although, in this case, the earlier psalms in the series referred primarily not to the temple itself, but to the pilgrim's departure. Even so, we saw that **Psalm 121** has a form that suggests multiple voices, in effect a kind of liturgy of departure. The pilgrim starts off in the first person:

> I lift up my eyes to the hills—
>   from where will my help come? (121:1)

Other voices then take up the liturgy, assuring the pilgrims of God's protection and affirming that God will bring them safely home:

> The Lord will keep
>   your going out and your coming in
>   from this time on and forevermore. (121:8)

Another Song of Ascents, **Psalm 132**, invites the pilgrims to relive imaginatively the moment when God took up residence in Zion. Perhaps it accompanied a re-enactment of the bringing of the Ark to Zion or at least a commemorative procession. This psalm may be too complex for the congregation as a whole to have joined in the singing, but they would at least be able to identify personally with the search it describes.

Psalm 132 invites pilgrims to relive imaginatively the story of the finding of the Ark, when God took up residence in Zion.

The text begins by recalling David's determination to make a place for God in his new capital. This is told in the third person, as a narrative:

> O LORD, remember in David's favor
>   all the hardships he endured;
> how he swore to the LORD
>   and vowed to the Mighty One of Jacob. . . . (132:1–2)

David's vow was that he would build a temple for God. What he first did, however, was to bring the Ark of the Covenant to Jerusalem and install it there in its tent-sanctuary.

In verse 6, the chorus suddenly shifts into first person plural, as if in excited recollection of having participated, themselves, in the finding of the Ark:

> We heard of it in Ephrathah;
>   we found it in the fields of Jaar. (132:6)

They recall their excited conversation at the thought of retrieving the ancient shrine of God's presence:

> "Let us go to his dwelling place;
>   let us worship at his footstool." (132:7)

It is a short, dramatic vignette reliving the story told in 2 Samuel 6 (minus the alarming fate of Uzzah). Through it, the pilgrims become, as it were, present at the very beginnings of the sanctuary of Zion. They even join in a prayer based on the one that traditionally accompanied the carrying of the Ark into battle, but with a twist. The old formula ran "Arise, O Lord, let your enemies be scattered." (Num 10:35) This time, the Ark is traveling not into battle, but to its true home:

> Rise up, O LORD, and go to your resting place,
>   you and the ark of your might. (132:8)

And the congregation, still in their role as the finders of the Ark, add two more prayers:

> Let your priests be clothed with righteousness,
>   and let your faithful shout for joy.
> For your servant David's sake
>   do not turn away the face of your anointed one. (132:9–10)

This reenactment begins in the earliest stages of Israel's covenant with God in the desert and concludes with the hope of a true and righteous heir for David. If it was written, as often thought, during the post-Exilic period, it expresses a hope for restoration of the long-lost monarchy.

After reciting God's promise to David (vv. 11–12), the psalm concludes with a response in God's own voice, promising God's eternal love for the temple, the city, and the people.

> "This is my resting place forever;
>   here I will reside, for I have desired it.
> I will abundantly bless its provisions;
>   I will satisfy its poor with bread.
> Its priests I will clothe with salvation,
>   and its faithful will shout for joy." (132:14–16)

The divine pronouncement concludes by promising a new offspring of David to preside over this era of prosperity and peace. The worshipper who had imaginatively joined the expedition to Jaar in search of the Ark is also given the opportunity to think of his or her own era as a time when God's good will for the people can be realized anew.

The Broad Scope of Hymns: Psalm 104

As we have said, a hymn consists of two elements, a summons to praise and a reason for praising. It is a simple plan that can accommodate an immense variety of themes. It can celebrate God's past graces or look forward in hope to the future. It can focus on God's generosity to the nation of Israel or look outward to the larger community of nations with a promise that they, too, can eventually be included in the worshipping community. It can concern itself with the human community or broaden its sweep to include the whole of creation—physical elements, animals, and spiritual beings.

Psalm 104 takes the whole world as its subject matter—a world in which humanity is just one more aspect of the vast and complex creation that God has made and delights in.

Psalm 104 is a superb example of this breadth of vision, emerging out of a highly personal, meditative stance of devotion. It summons to worship, not the public but only the singer's own heart and mind:

"Bless the LORD, O my soul." This does not mean that it could not have been used in the larger congregation, only that it begins by establishing a direct connection between the individual worshipper and God. From that starting point, it broadens out to take the whole world as its subject matter—a world in which humanity is just one more aspect of the vast and complex creation that God has made and delights in.

The catalogue of God's works begins in the heavens:

> You are clothed with honor and majesty,
>   wrapped in light as with a garment.
> You stretch out the heavens like a tent,
>   you set the beams of your chambers on the waters,
> you make the clouds your chariot,
>   you ride on the wings of the wind. . . . (104:1–3)

Descending to earth, the poet describes its creation out of the primeval waters in terms that recall the beginning of Genesis, but paint a more vivid picture:

> At your rebuke [the waters] flee;
>   at the sound of your thunder they take to flight.
> They rose up to the mountains, ran down to the valleys
>   to the place that you appointed for them.
> You set a boundary that they may not pass,
>   so that they might not again cover the earth. (104:7–9)

In this mythological cosmology, what kept the waters from flooding the earth was not some sort of "natural law," but the direct command of God.

Next, the poet moves on to the riches of nature: water, grass, wine, oil, the great forests that covered Lebanon and the wild animals that inhabited them. Our poet even takes up the wonders of the sea, a topic not much touched on by ancient Hebrew writers. This is not, however, a cleaned up, prettified view of nature. Our poet includes the carnivorous lion alongside the herbivorous cattle and wild goats and acknowledges that God, being the sole God and Creator, is giver of death as well as life:

> These all look to you
>   to give them their food in due season;

when you give it to them, they gather it up;
    when you open your hand, they are filled with good things.
When you hide your face, they are dismayed;
    when you take away their breath, they die
    and return to their dust.
When you send forth your spirit, they are created;
    and you renew the face of the ground. (104:27–30)

The idea of God as the creator of trouble as well as happiness, of death as well as life, is not a comfortable one. But it is not easy to avoid if one truly wants to maintain God's universality. Other psalms will struggle with these questions; the author of Psalm 104 simply looks with awe on the vastness of God's power and God's creative delight.

The poet finds delight even for one who is mortal in praising the eternal Maker:

May the glory of the LORD endure forever;
    may the LORD rejoice in his works. . . .
I will sing to the LORD as long as I live;
    I will sing praise to my God while I have my being. (104:31, 33)

The final lines of the psalm echo the beginning: "Bless the LORD, O my soul. Praise the LORD!"

Given all this rejoicing, the couplet just before these final lines may seem odd:

Let sinners be consumed from the earth,
    and let the wicked be no more. (104:35a)

But the sinners here are the exact opposite of the thankful soul that takes in and rejoices over the generosity of God in creation. Sin must eventually disappear from a perfected praise. And, from a modern perspective, scorn directed toward the created order surely has to be seen as a barrier to human communion with God.

Continuing the Conversation:

Many libraries have the multi-volume *Anchor Bible Dictionary*, which contains an article on "parallelism" and includes a discussion of the poetry of Psalms in the large article on "Psalms."

CHAPTER FOUR

"I Am Weary with My Crying"

Psalms of Lament, Trust, and Thanksgiving

The Many Functions of Lament: Psalm 69

Another important genre of psalm is the lament, which expresses distress over suffering and loss and asks for God's intervention. In contrast to the rather simple basic structure of the hymn, laments have as many as five basic elements: address to God; statement of the problem; request for help; affirmation of trust; and a vow to be fulfilled once the crisis is past. This is not a rigid formula. Any given lament may leave out some items or combine them in various ways. They may also add other elements such as confession of faults (or assertion of righteousness) and curses on one's enemies.

> Laments have as many as five basic elements: address to God; statement of the problem; request for help; affirmation of trust; and a vow to be fulfilled once the crisis is past.

Psalm 69 is a good example, since it presents the full formula at some length—and in brilliant poetry. The psalm scarcely pauses over its *address to God* before rushing urgently into telling about *the problem*:

> Save me, O God,
>> for the waters have come up to my neck.
> I sink in deep mire,
>> where there is no foothold;
> I have come into deep waters,
>> and the flood sweeps over me. (69:1–2)

This passage, capturing what it is like to be confronted by disaster, the sense of helplessness we feel when we can see no way out of a disastrous situation, has made this one of the best known psalms.

The image of the flood describes not the cause of trouble, but the speaker's sense of being overwhelmed by it. The actual occasion is an array of human enemies:

> More in number than the hairs of my head
>> are those who hate me without a cause;
> many are those who would destroy me,
>> my enemies who accuse me falsely.
> What I did not steal
>> must I now restore? (69:4)

The trouble is a legal attack, demanding restoration of something alleged to have been stolen.

To this, the speaker responds by asserting righteousness, though with a preliminary *confession:*

> O God, you know my folly;
>> the wrongs I have done are not hidden from you. (69:5)

The main point, however, is that there is no truth in this particular accusation. Indeed, the speaker insists that everything that was done was done for the sake of God and God's temple:

> It is for your sake that I have borne reproach,
>> that shame has covered my face.
> I have become a stranger to my kindred,
>> an alien to my mother's children.
> It is zeal for your house that has consumed me;
>> the insults of those who insult you have fallen on me. (69:7–9)

Thus the speaker suggests that this is a case of people who do not honor God attacking one whose principal offense is to be a devout worshipper. Worst of all, some of the attackers are the speaker's kin.

The *request for help* has been implicit all along, but now becomes more specific:

> But as for me, my prayer is to you, O LORD.
>> At an acceptable time, O God,
>>> in the abundance of your steadfast love, answer me.
>> With your faithful help rescue me
>>> from sinking in the mire;
>> let me be delivered from my enemies
>>> and from the deep waters.
>> Do not let the flood sweep over me,
>>> or the deep swallow me up,
>>> or the Pit close its mouth over me. (69:13–15)

For the speaker, the threat looks as serious as death itself. Even if death is not a literal threat here, to be dishonored publicly and cut off from networks of social support would have made life in the ancient city precarious.

At this point the psalm's *declaration of trust* follows. It is fleeting—so consumed is the speaker in recounting the troubles—but it is there:

> Answer me, O Lord, for your steadfast love is good;
>> according to your abundant mercy, turn to me. (69:16)

The psalmist can appeal to God, even in the midst of fear, because God is loving and merciful.

The social dimension of the attack now becomes the focus of the prayer, first in describing the wrongdoing of the enemies, who have succeeded in isolating the speaker from all support. Christians are familiar with this following passage in part from its use to describe Jesus' sufferings on the cross:

> Insults have broken my heart,
>> so that I am in despair.

For the speaker, the threat looks as serious as death itself. Even if death is not literally a threat, to be dishonored publicly and cut off from networks of social support would have made life in the ancient city precarious.

> I looked for pity, but there was none;
> and for comforters, but I found none.
> They gave me poison for food,
> and for my thirst they gave me vinegar to drink. (69:20–21)

The psalmist then uses the same social image, the meal, to pronounce a *curse* on the enemies:

> Let their table be a trap for them,
> a snare for their allies.
> Let their eyes be darkened so that they cannot see,
> and make their loins tremble continually.
> . . . .
> May their camp be a desolation;
> let no one live in their tents. (69:22–23, 25)

Their punishment will be to find themselves abandoned as completely as the speaker of the psalm.

Another interesting element comes fully into view here. The speaker may be under attack not only from these human enemies, but from God. Often people, then and now, interpret sickness as a sign that they have "done something wrong" or that they are being "punished." Our speaker mentioned earlier in the psalm that he had been fasting and wearing sackcloth, a sign of either mourning or penitence. Now we hear that the enemies

> . . . persecute those whom you have struck down,
> and those whom you have wounded, they attack still more.
> (69:26)

Perhaps the enemies have taken advantage of an illness to attack when it will be difficult to resist them.

Still, even in the depths of despair, the psalmist is confident enough to make *a vow* promising a song of thanksgiving when he recovers, a thank-offering that, the psalmist claims, will please God even more than an animal sacrifice. This public thanksgiving will encourage others to put their trust in God: "You who seek God, let your hearts revive." (vv. 30–33) The psalm then concludes with a brief version of such a thanksgiving psalm and a promise that God will save Zion and rebuild the cities of Judah (vv. 34–36).

This shift from individual to community may seem odd. It could perhaps have been added by later editors in order to give more general applicability to the psalm, making of it not only the appeal of an individual in deep trouble, but the appeal of the whole nation of Israel. But even without such an explanation, it makes a certain sense, for the welfare of the individual can never be separated completely from the welfare of the community. The psalm as it stands envisions the restoration of the needy person as part of God's good will not only toward one individual but toward a suffering place and people. Perhaps the title's ascription of this psalm to David is making the same point; by connecting the psalm to the king, even if there was no actual monarch at the time, the editor specified that it applied it to the life of the whole people.

Laments of King and Nation: Psalms 9, 80, 90

Many psalms of lament deal explicitly with the sorrows and sufferings of the nation, often personified in the "I" of the king. **Psalm 9**, for example, speaks in the royal voice, as becomes clear when we discover that the enemies against whom the psalm appeals are foreign nations. The psalm actually begins by describing, in hymnic style, how God has protected the speaker and "rebuked the nations."

> The enemies have vanished in everlasting ruins;
>> their cities you have rooted out;
>> the very memory of them has perished. (9:6)

Yet, all is not entirely well. There is still a threat:

> Be gracious to me, O LORD.
>> See what I suffer from those who hate me;
>> you are the one who lifts me up from the gates of death . . .
>> (9:13)

And the psalm concludes by calling on God to intervene:

> Rise up, O LORD! do not let mortals prevail;
>> let the nations be judged before you.
> Put them in fear, O LORD;
>> let the nations know that they are only human. (9:19–20)

The intervening verses express trust by speaking as if the desired salvation has already taken place:

> The nations have sunk in the pit that they made;
>> in the net that they hid has their own foot been caught.
> The LORD has made himself known, he has executed judgment;
>> the wicked are snared in the work of their own hands.
>> (9:15–16)

The way the psalm shifts from praise to appeal, from expression of trust to a cry for help, can be confusing if we read these different elements as sequential—one happening after the other. But they come together more easily if we understand that each segment is fulfilling a distinct requirement of the lament genre.

In other psalms, the nation speaks not through the "I" of the king, but in the plural "we." This is the case, for example, in **Psalm 80**. Some of its contents suggest that it was composed in the Northern Kingdom at about the time of its collapse under the Assyrian onslaught (722 or 721 BCE). Interestingly, it begins by calling on God as "Shepherd of Israel." "Shepherd," as we noted in the Introduction, was a common metaphor for "king" in the ancient Mediterranean world. God is the true king here, even though v. 17 will suggest that there may well be a human king, too, whom God is asked to help. The psalmist appeals to God:

Many psalms of lament deal explicitly with the sorrows and sufferings of the nation, often personified in the "I" of the king.

> You who are enthroned upon the cherubim, shine forth
>> before Ephraim, Benjamin and Manasseh.
> Stir up your might,
>> and come to save us! (80:1b–2)

The tribes of Ephraim, Benjamin, and Manasseh were central elements of the Northern Kingdom.

The psalmist reproaches God with having abandoned the people:

> You make us the scorn of our neighbors;
>> our enemies laugh among themselves. (80:6)

Yet, the plea continues, the people have always been dependent on God and have no other help. The psalmist tells a parable about the

Exodus from Egypt and entry into Canaan under the image of a vine that God had planted here:

> You brought a vine out of Egypt;
> you drove out the nations and planted it.
> You cleared the ground for it;
> it took deep root and filled the land. (80:8–9)

But now God has abandoned it:

> Why then have you broken down its walls,
> so that all who pass along the way pluck its fruit?
> The boar from the forest ravages it,
> and all that move in the field feed on it. (80:12–13)

The people plead with God to assume responsibility for them (and for their leader, modestly described simply as "the one at your right hand"):

> Turn again, O God of hosts;
> look down from heaven, and see;
> have regard for this vine,
> the stock that your right hand planted.
> They have burned it with fire, they have cut it down;
> may they perish at the rebuke of your countenance.
> But let your hand be upon the one at your right hand,
> the one whom you made strong for yourself. (80:14–17)

The "rebuke of your countenance" will be the severe, condemning frown that God casts on the Assyrians and their allies, enough to wither even the strongest of mortals. And the speakers of the lament acknowledge that they may have deserved it themselves and promise amendment of life:

> Then we will never turn back from you;
> give us life, and we will call on your name.
> Restore us, O LORD God of hosts;
> let your face shine, that we may be saved. (80:18–19)

It is striking that this psalm from the northern kingdom seems to have been incorporated with little alteration into the songbook of the

The opening verses of Psalm 90 form the inspiration for Isaac Watts's hymn "O God, our help in ages past."

Jerusalem temple. We are told that Hezekiah invited the remnants of the northern tribes to participate in the pilgrim feasts at Jerusalem (2 Chr 30); perhaps that is when it entered into the musical tradition there.

Psalm 90 is a lament attributed to Moses, who was also, like the kings later on, a kind of representative figure for the whole people, but the poem is framed in the voice of the community:

> Lord, you have been our dwelling place
> in all generations.
> Before the mountains were brought forth,
> or ever you had formed the earth and the world,
> from everlasting to everlasting you are God. (90:1–2)

The psalmist contrasts the eternity and power of God with the fragility of mortal human beings—as transient as the spring grass in an arid climate (vv. 5–6).

Yet, some particular suffering is in view here. Though it is never specified, the psalmist attributes it to God's anger over human sin:

> For we are consumed by your anger;
> by your wrath we are overwhelmed.
> You have set our iniquities before you,
> our secret sins in the light of your countenance.
> For all our days pass away under your wrath;
> our years come to an end like a sigh. (90:7–9)

At most, human life lasts seventy or eighty years, years filled with "toil and trouble." The psalmist appeals for relief from whatever additional trouble afflicts the people:

> Satisfy us in the morning with your steadfast love,
> so that we may rejoice and be glad all our days.
> Make us glad as many days as you have afflicted us,
> and as many years as we have seen evil. (90:14–15)

The particular beauty of this psalm consists in a sense of intimacy with God that can overcome the difference in power between humanity and the divine and can appeal to God's love even while acknowledging human inadequacy. The concluding prayer is both humble and passionate. It asks not simply to be rescued, but to regain the ability to build productive lives:

> Let the favor of the Lord our God be upon us,
>   and prosper for us the work of our hands—
> O prosper the work of our hands! (90:17)

Laments of Individuals: Psalms 28, 41

Individuals, too, brought their troubles before God in the temple, praying for protection and offering their declarations of faith in God. Sometimes the trouble had to do with illness, which made them doubly vulnerable. The simple fact of being unable to participate in public affairs meant that they became easy prey for rivals, but, in addition, sickness cast doubt on their virtue and integrity, further eroding their honor.

Illness could be interpreted as a divine judgement, making the sick doubly vulnerable. Being unable to participate in public affairs meant that they became easy prey for rivals, and sickness cast doubt on their virtue and integrity, further eroding their honor.

Psalm 41 is a good example. It begins with a statement of confidence:

> Happy are those who consider the poor;
>   the LORD delivers them in the day of trouble.
> The LORD protects them and keeps them alive;
>   they are called happy in the land.
>   You do not give them up to the will of their enemies.
> The LORD sustains them on their sickbed;
>   in their illness you heal all their infirmities. (41:1–3)

Several things are worth noticing here. One is the way the discourse shifts between third person ("The Lord delivers. . . The Lord sustains") and second ("You do not give them up. . . you heal"). The poet makes assertions about God's loving mercy and illustrates that truth by the freedom with which God can be addressed directly. The poet makes an assertion: If you have taken care of the poor, God will take care of you. And the poet follows it up by addressing God directly with a claim for assistance.

Having considered the poor does not mean that the psalmist is sinless. Indeed, the next step is a confession: "heal me, for I have sinned against you." But this is a brief and general confession. The real interest here is in detailing how wickedly the psalmist's enemies have acted. They speculate on when he will die. They come to visit on a pretext of bringing comfort, but actually to spy out the situation. They spread rumors. Even the speaker's closest friend has taken sides with them. The poet prays, "Raise me up, that I may repay them."

The concluding part of the psalm affirms the certainty of answered prayer:

> By this I know that you are pleased with me;
>> because my enemy has not triumphed over me.
> But you have upheld me because of my integrity,
>> and set me in your presence forever. (41:11–12)

The final verse of the psalm is the benediction that concludes Book I of the Psalter, though it can also be read as a triumphant assertion of God's assured response to the prayer.

Other laments, too, focus primarily on illness—for example, Psalms 38, 88, and 102. But the larger number of laments focus rather on the social dangers of life in the Ancient Near East. Indeed, as we have seen, even something as seemingly private as illness became a public event because it offered an opportunity for enemies to create other kinds of problems.

Psalm 28 is a relatively brief example. It begins with a great cry of anguish:

> To you, O Lord, I call;
>> my rock, do not refuse to hear me,
> for if you are silent to me,
>> I shall be like those who go down to the Pit. (28:1–2)

The Pit (i.e. the grave) puts a stop to human existence, for there is little hint in the Psalms of any belief in a resurrection or after-life. The present danger is thus a life-or-death issue for the speaker. Rather than describing it, however, the poet combines a description of the enemies with a prayer not to be confused with them or swept away with them in their just condemnation:

> Do not drag me away with the wicked,
>> with those who are workers of evil,

who speak peace with their neighbors,
    while mischief is in their hearts. (28:3)

The speaker asks God to "repay them according to their work," then turns, as it were, to the public as witnesses to proclaim that

Because they do not regard the works of the LORD,
    or the work of his hands,
he will break them down and build them up no more. (28:5)

Finally, the psalmist blesses God for the expected help and offers a song in celebration of assured deliverance. The concluding verses proclaim God as the strength not only of this one petitioner, but of all God's people:

The LORD is the strength of his people;
    he is the saving refuge of his anointed.
O save your people, and bless your heritage;
    be their shepherd, and carry them forever. (28:8–9)

Even the most individual and personal of troubles are seldom separated completely from concern for the larger community.

For other individual laments, see Psalms 38, 88, and 102.

Confession: Psalms 50, 51

We have noted that confession of fault is often part of laments. Some psalms of lament focus so strongly on this element that we can think of them as a distinct grouping. Indeed, they have long been known to Christian spirituality as the seven Penitential Psalms: 6, 32, 38, 51, 102, 130, and 143. This is not a clearly distinct genre. Psalms 38 and 143 are close to the standard lament in form, and Psalms 6 and 102 are in fact good examples of a lament for sickness. Psalm 130 we will treat in the following section as a Song of Trust. But, all in all, the element of penitence seems a little more to the fore in them. All are poems of no little power, marked by the intensity of intimate discourse. The psalmists are wrestling with their God.

Psalm 51 is the best known of these. Its title ascribes it to David after Nathan the prophet reproached him for his adultery with Bathsheba (2 Sam 12). That is the premier story of repentance in the Hebrew Scriptures, and the connection made with it tells us how highly the editors of the Psalter regarded this psalm. The two final verses suggest that it was actually written at a time when the walls of Jerusalem (and perhaps the temple as well) were in ruins. And the poet's claim to have sinned against God alone (v. 4) is hardly true for David, who had sinned quite seriously against both Bathsheba and her husband Uriah the Hittite—his own faithful commander.

This, however, takes nothing away from the psalm's power. It begins with a plea for forgiveness, framed in the language of purification:

> Have mercy on me, O God,
>   according to your steadfast love;
> according to your abundant mercy
>   blot out my transgressions.
> Wash me thoroughly from my iniquity,
>   and cleanse me from my sin. (51:1–2)

There is no precise list of sins, rather a general confession of sinfulness, framed in the language of hyperbole:

> Indeed, I was born guilty,
>   a sinner when my mother conceived me. (51:5)

The poet focuses on the sinner rather than the sin, at least partly because the psalm will go on to become a prayer for a transformed life:

> Create in me a clean heart, O God,
>   and put a new and right spirit within me.
> Do not cast me away from your presence,
>   and do not take your holy spirit from me. (51:10–11)

Note that NRSV does not capitalize "spirit" here, so as not to suggest that the psalmist is speaking of the Holy Spirit of Christian theology. Ideas of God's spirit in the Scriptures of Israel are less specific. In fact, God's court can be spoken of as containing many spirits (e.g., 1 Kings 22:1–23).

It is this transformed life, expressed in a song of praise and thanksgiving, that God desires:

> O Lord, open my lips,
>   and my mouth will declare your praise. (51:14)

There will be a psalm of thanksgiving, but our poet specifies that there will be no sacrifice—in contrast to Psalm 116:17–19, for example, which specifies both a psalm, calling "on the name of the LORD," and a sacrifice. For our psalmist, God wants not the sacramental sacrifice, but the sacrifice of self:

> The sacrifice acceptable to God is a broken spirit;
> a broken and contrite heart, O God, you will not despise. (51:17)

It does not follow that the psalmist wanted to abolish sacrifice. It is rather a matter of reconnecting it to its meaning. This is a perspective also found in Psalm 50. On the one hand, it accepts the rites of sacrifice as a norm. The voice of God is presented as saying,

> "Not for your sacrifices do I rebuke you;
> your burnt offerings are continually before me." (50:8)

But shortly afterward, the voice commends a more intimate and dynamic kind of relationship between worshipper and God:

> "If I were hungry, I would not tell you,
> for the world and all that is in it is mine.
> Do I eat the flesh of bulls,
> or drink the blood of goats?
> Offer to God a sacrifice of thanksgiving,
> and pay your vows to the Most High.
> Call on me in the day of trouble;
> I will deliver you, and you shall glorify me." (50:12–15)

Some scholars argue that the two concluding verses of Psalm 51 were added by another hand in order to counteract the impression given in verse 16 that God does not want sacrifices at the temple. It is possible, but hardly necessary. One can, after all, both maintain the rites of religion and call for the faithful to move through and beyond them into an active relationship with God.

Songs of Trust: Psalms 130, 131

The song of trust is another genre closely related to the lament and includes many of the best-loved psalms of all. Perhaps the supreme example is Psalm 23. As in a lament, a hint of danger hovers over it in

The genre of lament gave rise
to a related genre, the song
of trust, that includes many
of the best-loved psalms.

the reference to "the darkest valley" and "the ene-mies" who will have to be satisfied with being mere onlookers at the closing feast. The psalm of trust does not focus on the implied trouble, however, but on the speaker's relationship of trust with God.

The origin of these songs of trust in the lament is clearly dis-cernible in **Psalm 130**, which is also considered one of the penitential psalms. It begins with a memorable call for help:

> Out of the depths I cry to you, O LORD.
>   Lord, hear my voice!
> Let your ears be attentive
>   to the voice of my supplications! (130:1–2)

But there is no indication of the nature of the troubles; rather a hum-ble confession that no one is without sin, coupled with an assertion of confidence in God's mercy:

> If you, O LORD, should mark iniquities,
>   Lord, who could stand?
> But there is forgiveness with you,
>   so that you may be revered. (130:3–4)

This is already an expression of trust, amplified in the moving verses that follow:

> I wait for the LORD, my soul waits,
>   and in his word I hope;
> my soul waits for the Lord
>   more than those who watch for the morning,
>   more than those who watch for the morning. (130:5–6)

There is an intensity in the repetition of "wait" and "watch" here that is reminiscent of love poetry; indeed, the song of trust is a kind of love poem to God. The image of the night watch heightens the sense of expectation. The dawn will dispel the dangerous shadows where enemies can hide, and the watchers on the city wall will greet it with relief. But it is not unexpected. The watchers trust that, no matter how long the night seems, the morning will indeed come.

The conclusion of the psalm, like that of Psalm 28, broadens the scope of the poem from the individual petitioner to the whole people of Israel, making it particularly appropriate in its function as a "Song of Ascents," a pilgrim song:

The song of trust is a kind of love poem to God.

> O Israel, hope in the LORD!
>> For with the LORD there is steadfast love,
>> and with him is great power to redeem.
> It is he who will redeem Israel
>> from all its iniquities. (130:7–8)

The God who is ready to forgive sin is also ready to assist the people in all ways and is therefore worthy of trust.

We see the same kind of alternation of private and public in **Psalm 131** with its expression of trust as humility:

> O LORD, my heart is not lifted up,
>> my eyes are not raised too high;
> I do not occupy myself with things
>> too great and too marvelous for me. (131:1–2)

The poet embraces the calmness and quiet of a weaned child on its mother's breast and exhorts Israel to "hope in the LORD from this time on and forevermore."

Thanksgivings: Psalms 18, 30, 118

We have noted, in several of the laments, a promise to return to the temple with a song of thanks for God's help received. We have several examples of such thanksgivings in the Psalter. A particularly impressive one is **Psalm 118**, which seems to have accompanied a national celebration of military victory against some very threatening opponent. The "I" of this psalm sounds very much like the voice of the king. We have seen, however, that individual laments often included prayer for the whole people; it is not impossible, then, that the line between community and individual thanks-

The line between community and individual thanksgivings could become somewhat blurred and what began as an anthem for a public expression of thanksgiving could also serve more private occasions.

givings was also somewhat blurred and that what began as an anthem for public thanksgiving could also serve more private occasions.

The psalm begins with a summons to the congregation to join in God's praise and an assertion of God's faithfulness. Then we hear a poetic recitation of the events being celebrated:

> All nations surrounded me;
>> in the name of the LORD I cut them off!
> They surrounded me, surrounded me on every side;
>> in the name of the LORD I cut them off!
> They surrounded me like bees;
>> they blazed like a fire of thorns;
>> in the name of the LORD I cut them off!
> I was pushed hard, so that I was falling,
>> but the LORD helped me. (118:10–13)

The danger of the encounter is made vivid by the repetitions and the comparisons to attack by bees and to wildfire. It is almost as if we were seeing a motion picture of a prolonged and uncertain battle. But now, at last, "There are glad songs of victory in the tents of the righteous." (v. 15)

The speaker acknowledges that he was not without fault:

> The LORD has punished me severely,
>> but he did not give me over to death. (118:18)

Now the speaker begins a liturgical exchange with the assembled congregation, claiming the privilege of entering the temple to give thanks:

> Open to me the gates of righteousness,
>> that I may enter through them
>> and give thanks to the LORD.

The assembled throng responds:

> This is the gate of the LORD;
>> the righteous shall enter through it.

The king (to God):

> I thank you that you have answered me
> and have become my salvation.

The stone that the builders rejected
  has become the chief cornerstone. [Remember that he nearly
  lost the battle!]

Congregation:

This is the LORD's doing;
  it is marvelous in our eyes.
This is the day that the LORD has made;
  let us rejoice and be glad in it.
Save us, we beseech you, O LORD!
  O LORD, we beseech you, give us success! (118:19–25)

The congregation then concludes the psalm by welcoming the king:

Blessed is the one who comes in the name of the LORD.
  We bless you from the house of the LORD. (v. 26)

We even have a brief view of the sacrificial procession to the altar with garlands and branches (perhaps palm branches, a widespread ancient emblem of victory). A final thanksgiving formula and response round out the poem.

Psalm 18 gives a comparable example of a royal thanksgiving, though in this case the emphasis is on an extended (and somewhat bloody) description of the battle and victory. The struggle nearly ended in defeat:

The cords of death encompassed me;
  the torrents of perdition assailed me;
the cords of Sheol entangled me;
  the snares of death confronted me. (18:4–5)

God's intervention is described in terms of earthquake, storm clouds, hail, lightning, and thunder:

The earth reeled and rocked;
  the foundations also of the mountains trembled
  and quaked because he was angry.
Smoke went up from his nostrils
  and devouring fire from his mouth;
  glowing coals flamed forth from him. (18:7–8)

This is definitely an ancient warrior's vision of God, and the following description of how God helps the speaker would have been as intelligible to Homer's heroes as to the heroes of ancient Israel:

> He trains my hands for war,
>> so that my arms can bend a bow of bronze.
> You have given me the shield of your salvation,
>> and your right hand has supported me;
>> your help has made me great.
> You gave me a wide place for my steps under me,
>> and my feet did not slip.
> I pursued my enemies and overtook them;
>> and did not turn back until they were consumed. (18:34–37)

The modern reader can at least appreciate the splendor of the poetry, even if we are uneasy about so much gloating over the fallen.

In a more private vein, there are also psalms of thanksgiving for individuals. In **Psalm 30**, for example, the speaker gives thanks for deliverance from both foes and sickness:

> I will extol you, O LORD, for you have drawn me up,
>> and did not let my foes rejoice over me.
> O LORD my God, I cried to you for help,
>> and you have healed me. (30:1–2)

There follows a moving account of the speaker's trust in God, weakened for a time by troubles:

> As for me, I said in my prosperity,
>> "I shall never be moved."
> By your favor, O LORD,
>> you had established me as a strong mountain;
> you hid your face;
>> I was dismayed. (30:6–7)

The poet appealed to God:

> "What profit is there in my death,
>> if I go down to the Pit?
> Will the dust praise you?
>> Will it tell of your faithfulness"? (30:9)

Notice again here the presupposition that death is final and that there is no true afterlife. Even Sheol, like the Greek Hades, was at most a pale shadow of earthly life. For an even stronger statement, compare Psalm 6:5, one of the penitential psalms:

> For in death there is no remembrance of you;
> in Sheol who can give you praise? (6:5)

This presupposition makes God's renewal of life here and now still more striking, and our poet imagines it vividly:

> You have turned my mourning into dancing;
> you have taken off my sackcloth
> and clothed me with joy,
> so that my soul may praise you and not be silent.
> O LORD my God, I will give thanks to you forever. (30:11–12)

A Deer Longs for Flowing Streams: Psalms 42–43

There is material to sum up a whole lifetime's highs and lows in these psalms—laments, confessions, songs of trust, and thanksgivings. It is no surprise that so much of the most familiar material from the Psalter is found here. They embody in vivid form the challenges of human existence and also the experience of intimacy with God that has sustained so many people through great trials.

We began this chapter with a brief account of the form of a lament. But like the sonnet form in English, for example, this is a poetic convention that can incorporate diverse perspectives and surprise us with new insights. Not every lament is a simple filling out of the basic outline, and psalms that do not initially seem to fit the pattern perfectly may nonetheless be built on this foundation.

Psalms 42 and 43, which were almost certainly a single psalm that came to be divided through some confusion in copying, give us an example of the poetic potential of the lament. The opening image of a deer seeking water gives us an immediate grasp of the poet's sense of need and longing for God:

> As a deer longs for flowing streams,
> so my soul longs for you, O God.
> My soul thirsts for God,

for the living God.
When shall I come and behold
the face of God? (42:1–2)

The hymn "As pants the hart
[or deer] for cooling
streams" is a metrical version
of Psalm 42:1–7.

This is a daring request, for the tradition is that no one can behold God's face and live (Exod 33:17–23). The poet is claiming a level of profound intimacy with God.

The trouble that the poet laments is framed very briefly and almost indirectly:

My tears have been my food
day and night,
while people say to me continually,
"Where is your God?" (42:3)

The attack is not described in terms of the speaker's health or public status; it is framed as a religious insult. And it is related to the sanctuary, where the poet remembers:

how I went with the throng,
and led them in procession to the house of God,
with glad shouts and songs of thanksgiving,
a multitude keeping festival. (42:4)

Caught up in this memory, the poet cannot help mourning its loss.
But at the same time there is a self-exhortation (which will be repeated twice more in the poem) to maintain hope in God:

Why are you cast down, O my soul,
and why are you disquieted within me?
Hope in God; for I shall again praise him,
my help and my God. (42:5)

Loss of the public festivals and the reinforcement they gave to faith makes it difficult to maintain the sense of relationship with God. But the poet remembers God both as a God of great power and as a God who has implanted song in the soul:

Deep calls to deep
at the thunder of your cataracts;
all your waves and your billows

have gone over me.
By day the LORD commands his steadfast love,
and at night his song is with me,
a prayer to the God of my life. (42:7–8)

The psalm then repeats the lamentation over the taunting of the adversaries, who mock the failure, as they see it, of the psalmist's faith. It is like "a deadly wound in my body" (42:10). But again we hear the self-exhortation: "Why are you cast down?"

Only in the third iteration of this basic pattern does the poet appeal to God for vindication "against an ungodly people," a vindication described in terms of restoration to the worship of the sanctuary:

O send out your light and your truth;
let them lead me;
let them bring me to your holy hill
and to your dwelling.
Then I will go to the altar of God,
to God my exceeding joy;
and I will praise you with the harp,
O God, my God. (43:3–4)

There is no thirst for retaliation here, only hope for restoration in the future, as is confirmed by the third and final iteration of the self-exhortation, "Hope in God."

These two psalms are treasures of world literature as well as of Jewish and Christian spirituality. They speak of longing and of remembered joy, of hope and of a love that remains strong even when it seems that it cannot be fulfilled.

Continuing the Conversation:

The Psalms have been the single most important inspiration of Christian lyric poetry—not surprisingly, given that Christians have been praying them and singing them all these centuries. In the sixteenth and seventeenth centuries, metrical versions of them were created to be sung in churches, and many survive in modern hymnals. But even more important is the way they pervaded original poetry. There is probably no better example than the poems of George Herbert, but anthologies of Christian verse will generally provide many others.

CHAPTER FIVE

"The Heavens Are Telling the Glory of God"

Psalms of Wisdom

Reflecting on God and the World: Psalm 19

The preceding chapters have focused on psalms that give direct expression to the human relationship with God—in praise or in lament, in declarations of trust or thanksgiving. Another important element in the Psalter is what scholars refer to as "wisdom." Wisdom, in the context of ancient Israel, was a tradition of reflecting on the whole range of human experience. It could touch on things as seemingly mundane as good table manners (Sirach 32), or it could tackle the most profound issues of theodicy (Job). It was interested in what we would call "nature" in modern English, and it was equally interested in what we call "ethics." These were not separate and distinct categories in ancient Hebrew literature; they were all gathered together as worthy subjects of reflection under the heading of "wisdom."

> "Wisdom" in ancient Israel reflected on the whole range of human experience—from good table manners to theodicy, from nature to ethics.

Psalm 19 is a beautiful example of a psalm that embodies this sort of wisdom, offering personal reflection on the widest range of human experience. It begins by expressing wonder at the universe:

> The heavens are telling the glory of God;
>   and the firmament proclaims his handiwork. (19:1)

The poet personifies day and night by placing them in mutual conversation:

> Day to day pours forth speech,
>   and night to night declares knowledge. (19:2)

They sound like a group of elders sharing news and interpretation with one another at the town gate. The image is a playful one, but the psalmist insists that there is a reality in it—something the reverent observer will be able to perceive:

> There is no speech nor are there words;
>   their voice is not heard;
> yet their voice goes out through all the earth,
>   and their words to the end of the world. (19:3–4)

The universe our poet imagined, of course, was the old Babylonian cosmology that we have encountered in other psalms—the earth as a flat space at the center, surrounded by the waters and covered with the crystalline dome of the firmament. The sun, in this universe, literally rose at the eastern edge and set at the western edge of the earth. But our poet is focused less on contemporary science than on the life-giving power of the sun, personified as a bridegroom, a hero in his prime, dancing his way from one end of the heavens to the other and warming the earth below. Even allowing for the vast distance between this ancient cosmology and ours, we can recognize in these images our common human delight in the natural world and the pleasure we take at the sun's warming return after a cold night.

The opening verses of Psalm 19 were the inspiration for Joseph Addison's hymn "The spacious firmament on high."

Then the psalmist takes an unexpected turn:

> The law *[torah]* of the LORD is perfect,
>   reviving the soul . . . (19:7a)

And the poet continues by assembling a series of synonyms for the religion of Torah:

> the *decrees* of the LORD are sure,
>   making wise the simple;
> the *precepts* of the LORD are right,
>   rejoicing the heart;
> the *commandment* of the LORD is clear,
>   enlightening the eyes;
> the *fear* of the LORD is pure,
>   enduring forever;
> the *ordinances* of the LORD are true
>   and righteous altogether. (19:7b-9)

The psalm celebrates the study of God's commandments in Torah with the same enthusiasm and warmth that characterized its earlier appreciation of the glories of the heavens:

> More to be desired are they than gold,
>   even much fine gold;
> sweeter also than honey,
>   and drippings of the honeycomb. (19:10)

There is no separation here between acknowledgement of God in the experience of nature and reverence for God in the practice of religion. Wisdom draws all of human experience into the contemplation of God's work.

Study of Torah necessarily includes the ethical dimension of human life, and our poet goes on to pray for self-understanding. Torah warns us against our faults, but no one is completely conscious of one's own sins. Accordingly, the psalmist prays God to preserve us from our tendency to err. NRSV has an alternative translation in a footnote to verse 13 that fits the flow of the poem better than the translation in the text:

> Keep back your servant also *from proud thoughts;*
>   do not let them have dominion over me. (19:13)

Protection from the insolent, as in the text of NRSV, is certainly worth praying for, as we have seen elsewhere in the Psalms. But this psalm is turning our attention inward toward our own motives and intentions and the way they correspond (or fail to correspond) with both the wonders of creation and the admonitions of Torah.

This is exactly the point made in the famous closing prayer:

> Let the words of my mouth and the meditation of my heart
> be acceptable to you,
> O LORD, my rock and my redeemer. (19:14)

Thus, a psalm that begins in the farthest reaches of creation ends in the heart, asking that our inmost meditations may be brought into line with the wonder and generosity that God shows us in nature and in revelation.

If we look back over this psalm, we can see that it has elements of poetic genres we identified earlier. It opens in hymnic form, celebrating God's glory. The praise of Torah in verses 7–10 has much in common with the psalms of trust. The confession and request for protection in verses 11–14 remind us of the lament. Wisdom psalms are distinguished, in fact, not by a single format but by their breadth of interests and reflective mode. They express a meditative perspective on the variety of ways in which faith in God intersects with daily human experience.

Celebrating the Creator: Psalms 65, 104

Reverence for God's work in creation is a pervasive theme in the Psalms. In one sense, this is not surprising. In the time when they were written, most people lived and worked in a world of small cities and towns closely inter-related with the croplands, steppes, and desert around them. Wilderness was a place where people retreated to fast and pray or to seek refuge from enemies. It did not have the connotation of remoteness and rarity that it has in our more crowded and urban world; it was a reality of ordinary life. And because people were directly engaged with the natural world, there was less sense of humanity as standing over against nature. Instead, the Psalms often express a sense of parallelism between us and the other creatures.

In the world of the psalmists, wilderness was a place where people retreated to fast and pray or to seek refuge from enemies. It was a reality of ordinary life, and there was less sense of humanity as standing over against nature.

Psalm 104, which we looked at earlier, is perhaps the very best example. It celebrates, in hymnic style, God's concern for the whole of creation:

> You cause the grass to grow for the cattle,
>   and plants for people to use,
> to bring forth food from the earth,
>   and wine to gladden the human heart,
> oil to make the face shine,
>   and bread to strengthen the human heart. (104:14–15)

The very order of the universe serves the diversity of creatures:

> You make darkness, and it is night,
>   when all the animals of the forest come creeping out.
> The young lions roar for their prey,
>   seeking their food from God.
> When the sun rises, they withdraw
>   and lie down in the their dens.
> People go out to their work
>   and to their labor until the evening. (104:20–23)

In contrast to the human-centeredness of modern culture, which is only just beginning to recognize that usefulness to *us* is not the only measure of value in the world, the psalmist is prepared to accept that God may have formed the other animals for their own sake— out of sheer creative delight:

> O Lord, how manifold are your works!
>   In wisdom you have made them all;
>   the earth is full of your creatures.
> Yonder is the sea, great and wide,
>   creeping things innumerable are there,
>   living things both small and great.
> There go the ships,
>   and Leviathan that you formed to sport in it. (104:24–26)

We tend to assume that "Leviathan" means "whale." After all, its description in Job 41 emphasizes its size—though, all in all, it sounds more like a crocodile. But I wonder if our poet was thinking of porpoises, which are certainly to be found in the Mediterranean. "Sporting" sounds very like what a porpoise does.

This is not to say that the psalmists were all early environmentalists. They were quite interested in the pragmatic issue of how the natural world sustained human populations—not something that could be taken for granted in a world that had limited ability to transport goods in bulk and was therefore more vulnerable to famine than ours. **Psalm 65** is a hymn celebrating the *abundance* of the creation. The harvest is its ultimate focus, but it begins in the temple, with praise of God and delight in worship:

> Praise is due to you,
>   O God, in Zion;
> and to you shall vows be performed,
>   O you who answer prayer!
> To you all flesh shall come. (65:1–2)

The middle section of the psalm focuses on God's power as expressed both in the majesty of creation and in God's protection of Israel:

> You silence the roaring of the seas,
>   the roaring of their waves,
>   the tumult of the peoples.
> Those who live at earth's farthest bounds are awed by your signs;
>   you make the gateways of the morning and evening shout for
>   joy. (65:7–8)

Here, as in Psalm 104, no sharp distinction is made between humanity and the rest of the creation, though the non-human orders may come more easily to their rejoicing before God than humanity, distracted as it is by its perennial wars and hostilities.

The psalm reaches its goal with the celebration of rain and the ensuing agricultural abundance:

> You visit the earth and water it,
>   you greatly enrich it;
> the river of God is full of water;
>   you provide the people with grain,
>   for so you have prepared it.

You water its furrows abundantly,
    settling its ridges,
softening it with showers,
    and blessing its growth. (65:9–10)

The farmers of ancient Israel depended on precipitation, not irrigation. The "river of God" is the water above the firmament, the source
of rain and snow. Egypt may have the Nile—and
the attendant labors of irrigation; Israel has the   *The farmers of ancient Israel*
river of God. The rain brings abundant crops; the   *depended on precipitation,*
wagon-tracks carry a long procession of carts haul-   *not irrigation. Egypt may*
ing them to storage. And "the pastures of the   *have the Nile—and the atten-*
                                                       dant labors of irrigation;
wilderness," the seasonal grasses of the steppe, sup- *Israel has the river of God.*
port large flocks of sheep. If the psalmist goes on to
project human joy onto the hills that "gird themselves with joy" and
valleys that "shout and sing together for joy," who can complain?

Reflecting on Humanity: Psalms 8, 33, 146

The psalmists see the human creature as a compound of weakness
and strength. **Psalm 8** begins, in hymnic style, by exalting God's
power:

O LORD, our Sovereign,
    how majestic is your name in all the earth! (8:1)

It goes on to observe how puny humanity is in comparison with
God's greatest creations:

When I look at your heavens, the work of your fingers,
    the moon and the stars that you have established;
what are human beings that you are mindful of them,
    mortals that you care for them? (8:3–4)

And yet, God has chosen to share with us some of God's own power
and authority:

Yet you have made them a little lower than God,
    and crowned them with glory and honor.
You have given them dominion over the works of your hands;
    you have put all things under their feet. . . . (8:5–6)

95

The emphasis on a kind of dual nature in humanity is reminiscent of Genesis 2, where God creates Adam from the dust of the earth and God's own breath.

This does not mean that humanity is invincible. **Psalm 33** insists that God remains in charge and that human fortunes are basically unpredictable:

> The LORD brings the counsel of the nations to nothing;
>   he frustrates the plans of the peoples. (33:10)

> A king is not saved by his great army;
>   a warrior is not delivered by his great strength. (33:16)

Humanity, for all its greatness, remains fundamentally vulnerable.

In the same vein, **Psalm 146** contrasts its praise of God's power and faithfulness with a caution about overconfidence in human leaders:

> Do not put your trust in princes,
>   in mortals, in whom there is no help.
> When their breath departs, they return to the earth;
>   on that very day their plans perish. (146:3–4)

The point is not, it seems, to dismiss political realities—much less to dismiss the importance of justice in public affairs. It is rather to form a realistic (and therefore not unbounded) estimate of what human leaders can succeed in accomplishing.

The Law of God: Psalms 78, 119

One key element in the faith of the psalmists is that the creator of the universe and the God who chose Israel are one and the same God. Accordingly, they are as interested in Israel's national history as in the larger creation. **Psalm 78** offers an extended commentary on that history from the Exodus and the wilderness wandering to the conquest of Canaan and the ensuing triumphs and disasters of the nation there. It concludes with God's choosing of Jerusalem and the line of David. The culminating point of the story seems to be the linking of the sanctuary of Zion and the Davidic monarchy:

> He built his sanctuary like the high heavens,
>   like the earth, which he has founded forever.

He chose his servant David,
    and took him from the sheepfolds. . . (78:69–70)

Here a writer in the reflective wisdom tradition offers an interpretation of Israel's history that both affirms the faithfulness of God and warns against any failure to remain committed to the law that God has commanded.

Deuteronomic theology saw Israelite history as a repeating pattern of forgetfulness and unfaithfulness on the part of Israel, which provoked divine punishment, followed by a temporary return to faithfulness.

The psalm tells the story not in chronological order, but in a thematic way, contrasting episodes that embody God's generosity with those that provoke the divine wrath. This is reminiscent of Deuteronomic theology, which saw Israelite history as a repeating pattern of forgetfulness and unfaithfulness on the part of Israel, which then provoked divine punishment, followed by a temporary return to faithfulness. This is a story punctuated with great acts of salvation on God's part, but even these cannot long hold their place in the people's memory. The retrieval of memory is the psalmist's great theme:

Give ear, O my people, to my teaching;
    incline your ears to the words of my mouth.
I will open my mouth in a parable;
    I will utter dark sayings from of old,
things that we have heard and known,
    that our ancestors have told us.
We will not hide them from their children;
    we will tell to the coming generation
the glorious deeds of the LORD, and his might,
    and the wonders that he has done. (78:1–4)

Notice the emphasis on teaching the story of the past, not simply as information, but as parable and "dark sayings," which must be contemplated and puzzled over and understood before the life of the people can thrive in covenant with God.

God established "a law in Israel"—
which he commanded our ancestors
    to teach to their children;
that the next generation might know them,

the children yet unborn,
and rise up and tell them to their children. . . . (78:5–6)

Then the poet turns to an account of failures and disasters, each framed in terms of a forgetful people who cannot remember God's earlier works on their behalf:

They forgot what he had done,
and the miracles that he had shown them.
In the sight of their ancestors he worked marvels
in the land of Egypt, in the fields of Zoan.
He divided the sea and let them pass through it,
and made the waters stand like a heap. (78:11–13)

Or again:

How often they rebelled against him in the wilderness
and grieved him in the desert!
They tested God again and again,
and provoked the Holy One of Israel.
They did not keep in mind his power,
or the day when he redeemed them from the foe;
when he displayed his signs in Egypt,
and his miracles in the fields of Zoan. (78:40–43)

Some of the disasters that followed on this forgetfulness had human agents—the foes who defeated Ephraim (i.e. the northern kingdom) in battle (v. 9) or who destroyed the temple at Shiloh (vv. 60–61). Others were the direct work of God, such as the plague that killed the people in the wilderness (vv. 30–31). But God was behind all of them, punishing the people for their failure to remember and their betrayal of the covenant.

Nonetheless, the psalmist insists that God's gracious purpose continued:

Yet he, being compassionate,
forgave their iniquity,
and did not destroy them;
often he restrained his anger,
and did not stir up all his wrath.

He remembered that they were but flesh,
    a wind that passes and does not come again. (78:38–39)

We could say that the psalmist here is developing a theology of history. It looks the brutal realities of it in the face and finds meaning in them—even hope for the future—by showing how they can be understood as part of a dynamic relationship with God.

The psalm ends with hope centered on Zion and the Davidic dynasty, suggesting that it was composed after the destruction of the northern kingdom of Israel, perhaps in the reign of Hezekiah or during the great national revival of religion under Josiah, when the influence of Deuteronomy was important. The poet of Psalm 78 has laid out the argument at considerable length (second only to Psalm 119). But we also find much the same perspective represented more briefly in Psalm 81.

> *The psalmist's theology of history looks the brutal realities of history in the face and finds meaning in them—even hope for the future—by showing how they can be understood as part of a dynamic relationship with God.*

The importance of Torah continued to increase after the destruction of Jerusalem by the Chaldeans, for the institutions of temple and kingship were no longer available to embody and support the nation's identity. The high valuation the editors of the Psalms placed on it is particularly evident in the very long **Psalm 119**, a series of meditations on love of Torah, constructed in the form of an alphabetical acrostic. NRSV, unfortunately, has omitted any indication of the acrostic, but it does retain the division of the text into stanzas of eight verses each. In Hebrew, each verse of the first stanza begins with the letter *aleph*, those of the second stanza with *beth*, and so forth. Acrostics were not uncommon in ancient poetry and are found here and there in other psalms. Some of these appear to be incomplete, but one other, Psalm 145, also makes its way through the entire Hebrew alphabet, one verse to each letter. The purpose of such acrostics may have been to aid memorization or to provide a check for copyists. But perhaps the strongest attraction in them was the sense of completeness and wholeness they provided to the process of composition.

> *Perhaps the strongest attraction in alphabetic acrostics was the sense of completeness and wholeness they provided to the process of composition.*

Psalm 119 weaves each of its stanzas around a series of synonyms for the religion of Torah (not unlike what we encountered in Psalm 19): law, decrees, precepts, statutes, commandments, and ordinances—and a few other terms used less regularly. The *aleph* stanza opens the whole poem with a benediction on the faithful:

> Happy are those whose way is blameless,
>> who walk in the law of the LORD.
> Happy are those who keep his decrees,
>> who seek him with their whole heart,
> who also do no wrong,
>> but walk in his ways. (119:1–3)

The poet prays to be one of these blessed souls:

> O that my ways may be steadfast
>> in keeping your statutes!
> Then I shall not be put to shame,
>> having my eyes fixed on all your commandments. (119:5–6)

The commandments are seen as the prescription for a healthy society and for responsible behavior in that context—which is the classic understanding of Torah in the wisdom tradition.

At the end of the first stanza, another element appears—one that will recur throughout this psalm—an element drawn from lament. The poet expects that life will not always go well for the faithful believer and prays for God's protection:

> I will observe your statutes;
>> do not utterly forsake me. (119:8)

The speaker of the poem notes elsewhere that "I live as an alien in the land" (v. 19) and is in danger from those who neglect Torah. Hence the appeal for help:

> You rebuke the insolent, accursed ones,
>> who wander from your commandments;
> take away from me their scorn and contempt,
>> for I have kept your decrees.
> Even though princes sit plotting against me,
>> your servant will meditate on your statutes. (119:21–23)

This suggests the Exile or the post-Exilic period as the time of composition for Psalm 119—a time of political fragility even for those who had returned, with imperial authorization, to rebuild Jerusalem and the temple. It was also the time when the Torah became broadly available as a particular object of study among the devout, as it has remained ever since. Neither the rebuilding of the city and temple nor the new formulation of Torah was without opponents, whether from surrounding ethnic groups or even within the remnants of Israel and Judah.

The note of danger and the appeal for God's help and defense become more intense toward the end of Psalm 119 alongside a growing intensity in the expression of love for Torah. We read:

> Your decrees are wonderful;
> > therefore my soul keeps them.
> The unfolding of your words gives light;
> > it imparts understanding to the simple.
> With open mouth I pant,
> > because I long for your commandments. (119:129–31)

And alongside this passion, we find great anxiety:

> Those who persecute me with evil purpose draw near;
> > they are far from your law. (119:150)

> Many are my persecutors and my adversaries,
> > yet I do not swerve from your decrees. (119:157)

> Princes persecute me without cause,
> > but my heart stands in awe of your words. (119:161)

The Human Community: Psalms 14, 15, 53

The first person singular, the "I," that speaks in Psalm 119 might give the impression that enthusiasm for Torah was the preserve of isolated individuals, but that would be misleading. The deep commitment of the individual was indeed an ideal, but Torah was always seen as a guide for the authentic life of the whole community, something to be upheld by all faithful citizens. When **Psalm 15** asks who the truly religious are, it poses the question in terms of admission to the sanctuary, but it answers in terms not of belief or ritual correctness, but of social ethics:

> O Lord, who may abide in your tent?
>> Who may dwell on your holy hill?
> Those who walk blamelessly, and do what is right,
>> and speak the truth from their heart;
> who do not slander with their tongue,
>> and do no evil to their friends,
>> nor take up a reproach against their neighbors . . . (15:1–3)

They not only model their own life in this way, but they expect the like of those around them, despising the wicked and honoring "those who fear the Lord." (v. 4)

> *When Psalm 15 asks who the truly religious are, it poses the question in terms of admission to the sanctuary, but it answers in terms not of belief or ritual correctness, but of social ethics.*

Psalm 14 (and **Psalm 53**, which as we noted, is almost identical) makes the same point in negative form, accusing those who do evil of implicitly denying God. (It also pessimistically asserts that they are the great majority.)

> Fools say in their hearts, "There is no God."
>> They are corrupt, they do abominable deeds;
>> there is no one who does good.
> The Lord looks down from heaven on humankind
>> to see if there are any who are wise,
>> who seek after God.
> They have all gone astray, they are all alike perverse;
>> there is no one who does good,
>> no, not one.
> Have they no knowledge, all the evildoers
>> who eat up my people as they eat bread,
>> and do not call upon the Lord? (14:1–4)

The psalmist does not have in view modern atheists, who object to the idea of God on intellectual grounds and who, like those who claim to be believers, may or may not be moral people. In the psalmist's day, virtually everyone participated in religious rites. The fool is, rather, the person who has decided to act as if the rites were a pious sham and justice was irrelevant. The real issue of atheism, for the poet, is less a matter of belief than of behavior. In fact, belief here is deduced from behavior.

> *The real issue of atheism, for Psalm 14, is less a matter of belief than of behavior. Indeed, it deduces the fools' unbelief from their oppression of others.*

Questioning God: Psalms 39, 49, 73

Psalms 14 and 15 agree that God will reward the faithful and punish the wicked. Of the righteous, the one says:

> Those who do these things shall never be moved. (15:5)

Of the wicked, the other says:

> There they shall be in great terror,
>   for God is with the company of the righteous. (14:5)

But these claims are problematic, for in reality the righteous do not always flourish nor the wicked suffer. Psalm 14 effectively admits as much by concluding with a prayer:

> O that deliverance for Israel would come from Zion!
>   When the LORD restores the fortunes of his people,
>   Jacob will rejoice; Israel will be glad. (14:7)

This kind of justice is a future hope for the poet, not a present reality.

There are psalmists who struggle quite directly with this problem and, like the author of Job, another great wisdom poet, raise the question of God's justice. **Psalm 39** is a lament, asking God to relieve the speaker of an undeserved suffering. Since the speaker, whatever his sins may be, perceives himself as fundamentally one of the faithful and upright, his suffering poses a challenge to faith. He cannot even speak in the presence of the wicked because they will turn his sufferings back on him in mockery:

> I said, "I will guard my ways
>   that I may not sin with my tongue;
> I will keep a muzzle on my mouth
>   as long as the wicked are in my presence." (39:1)

The poet begs God not to "make me the scorn of the fool" (v. 8), but seems to fear that God may actually be indifferent, that mortals do not mean much to the divine:

> Surely everyone stands as a mere breath.   *Selah*
>> Surely everyone goes about like a shadow.
> Surely for nothing they are in turmoil;
>> they heap up, and do not know who will gather. (39:5–6)

We may well be reminded of some of the more pessimistic passages in another wisdom book, Ecclesiastes (e.g., chapter 2).

Still the poet does claim a certain relationship with God:

> "Hear my prayer, O LORD,
>> and give ear to my cry;
>> do not hold your peace at my tears.
> For I am your passing guest,
>> an alien, like all my forebears.
> Turn your gaze away from me, that I may smile again,
>> before I depart and am no more." (39:12–13)

The poet of Psalm 39 seems to fear that God may be indifferent, that the fate of mortals may not mean much to the divine. The Psalms include expressions of doubt alongside those of faith.

We have perhaps no more vivid illustration of the breadth of perspective the Psalms embrace than this request to be *let alone* by God. It is, in part, simply an expression of extreme humility—the least thing one could possibly ask. But, if taken literally, it stands in sharp contrast to the many Psalms that emphatically request God's active involvement.

We find a more extended (and theologically nuanced) treatment of the problem of justice in **Psalm 73**, which begins by reasserting the orthodoxy that "God is good to the upright" (1), but goes on to admit doubts:

> But as for me, my feet had almost stumbled;
>> my steps had nearly slipped.
> For I was envious of the arrogant;
>> I saw the prosperity of the wicked. (73:2–3)

The idea of a future life where such problems could be set right is rare within the Scriptures of Israel. In fact, we have seen the poets of Psalms 6, 30, and 115 state the opposite as a known truth.

Our psalmist, accordingly, finds that the prosperity of the wicked calls into question the assurance of Psalms 14 and 15 that both righteous and wicked will alike receive what they deserve:

> They set their mouths against heaven,
>   and their tongues range over the earth.
> Therefore the people turn and praise them,
>   and find no fault in them.
> And they say, "How can God know?
>   Is there knowledge in the Most High?" (73:9–11)

This has created bitter distress for the psalmist, a condition reversed only by a revelation reaffirming God's judgment on the wicked and care for the righteous—a revelation received in the temple itself:

> . . . when I thought how to understand this,
>   it seemed to me a wearisome task,
> until I went into the sanctuary of God;
>   then I perceived their end.
> Truly you set them in slippery places;
>   you make them fall to ruin. (73:16–18)

The psalmist is now able to confess that disbelief was wrong and return to faith:

> When my soul was embittered,
>   when I was pricked in heart,
> I was stupid and ignorant;
>   I was like a brute beast toward you.
> Nevertheless I am continually with you:
>   you hold my right hand.
> You guide me with your counsel,
>   and afterward you will receive me with honor. (73:21–24)

To some degree, the sense of God's intimate presence and friendship, gained in the temple, allows the psalmist to live with the reality of an

Psalm 73:24 may be alluding to a still-new teaching that, for the righteous, life continues with God after death.

imperfect justice in this world. It is also possible, however, that the second part of v. 24 ("afterward you will receive me with honor") alludes to a still-new teaching that life continues with God after death for the righteous. If so, it was perhaps an esoteric teaching imparted only to the few, which makes the psalmist reluctant to do anything more here than allude to it.

Psalm 49, though it is a very pessimistic meditation on the universality of death, may perhaps contain a hint of the same doctrine. True, all alike must die:

> Like sheep they are appointed for Sheol;
>> Death shall be their shepherd;
> straight to the grave they descend,
>> and their form shall waste away;
>> Sheol shall be their home. (49:14)

But the poet at least hints at the possibility of an exception:

> But God will ransom my soul from the power of Sheol,
>> for he will receive me.   *Selah* (49:15)

The phrase could mean simply that God will rescue the poet from some imminent threat of death, but in the context of the psalm as a whole, it seems more likely that it alludes to a hope of life after death.

The Ethos of Justice: Psalm 101

Regardless of whether individual righteousness is rewarded or not, the wisdom tradition was interested in the principles of civic integrity. Justice is held up as the ultimate duty of government—often, as we saw in Chapter 2, with specific reference to the king,

Psalm 101 is framed as a first-person declaration of intentions:

> I will sing of loyalty and of justice;
>> to you, O LORD, I will sing.
> I will study the way that is blameless.
>> When shall I attain it? (101:1–2)

The scope of what follows suggests that the speaker could only be a king. Who else could say:

One who secretly slanders a neighbor
    I will destroy.
A haughty look and an arrogant heart
    I will not tolerate.
I will look with favor on the faithful in the land,
    so that they may live with me;
whoever walks in the way that is blameless
    shall minister to me. (101:5–6)

The psalms' insistence on righteousness and justice is thus a matter of creating a just and livable social order with special concern for the poor and those with the least ability to defend themselves. Only a commonwealth governed by such a standard can hope for genuine prosperity.

> *Righteousness is a matter of creating a just and livable social order with special concern for the poor and those with the least ability to defend themselves. Only a commonwealth governed by such a standard can hope for genuine prosperity.*

Openness to the Larger World: Psalm 67

The psalmists' sense of justice and uprightness is closely tied to the Torah, the specific law of Israel. But they were also heirs to an ancient wisdom tradition that was not exclusive to any one nation. We know wisdom writings from ancient Egypt and Mesopotamia, and even in the Hebrew Scriptures we find wisdom credited to non-Israelite authors (the collections of sayings found in Proverbs 30–31) and featuring non-Israelite speakers (the book of Job). The Psalter, too, is not without a broader vision of wisdom in the world and its peoples.

Psalm 67 begins by celebrating Israel's particular connection with God:

May God be gracious to us and bless us
    and make his face to shine upon us,   *Selah*
that your way may be known upon earth,
    your saving power among all nations. (67:1–2)

The prosperity of Israel will be the best indication to others that God's way is a way of peace and prosperity on earth. At the same time, the psalmist invites all the nations to join in the praise of God, precisely because they, too, will be judged by God. This is not presented as a threat, but as something that the Gentiles can understand and respect—as good news, in other words:

> Let the nations be glad and sing for joy,
>> for you judge the peoples with equity
>> and guide the nations upon earth. (67:4)

This perspective reflects the conviction found in Psalm 104 that God, as creator, is God of the whole earth and all its peoples. And this expanding of the horizon to the larger world is one of the wisdom tradition's great contributions to the Psalms and to the scriptures in general.

Continuing the Conversation:

A recent work emphasizing the value of the Psalter for a renewed understanding of the environment and our part in it is Arthur Walker-Jones, *The Green Psalter: Resources for an Ecological Spirituality* (Minneapolis: Fortress Press, 2009).

For a brief introduction to wisdom literature, see the article "Wisdom in the OT" in the *Anchor Bible Dictionary*.

CHAPTER SIX

"One Generation Shall Laud Your Works to Another"

The Ongoing Influence of the Psalms

Psalms Beyond the Psalter

The writing of psalms did not cease simply because the Psalter came into official use. They continued to be produced and used for a long time. And, indeed, they have continued to inspire poets of faith ever since.

One early addition to psalmic literature became part of the Orthodox Church's canon of the Old Testament and is included in the NRSV translation of the Apocrypha as Psalm 151. Its title ascribes it to David "after he had fought in single combat with Goliath" and also acknowledges that "it is outside the number"—that is, the one hundred fifty psalms that make up the canonical Psalter. It was long known only in the ancient Greek translation, but in more recent times a copy of it in Hebrew was found among the Qumran documents, where other examples of the ongoing vitality of psalm-writing may also be found. If Psalm 151 reads a bit disjointedly, we now know that it was in fact made up out of fragments of two separate psalms that appear in the Qumran document.

Other psalm-like poems are scattered through the scriptures, including the Apocrypha and the Gospel of Luke. Many have entered into Christian worship as canticles in Morning and Evening Prayer.

Other psalm-like poems are scattered through the Hebrew Scriptures, including such examples as the Songs of Moses and Miriam (Exod 15), the Thanksgiving of Hannah (1 Sam 2), the song of David (2 Sam 22, very similar to Ps 18), and the whole Book of Lamentations. There are yet more examples in the Apocrypha, such as the prayer of Sirach (Sir 51) and the Prayer of Azariah and the Song of the Three Jews in the fiery furnace (found in the Greek, but not the Hebrew form of the Book of Daniel). The Song of the Three Jews (the well-known Shadrach, Meshach, and Abednego) appears in Anglican liturgy divided into the two canticles *Benedictus es, Domine* ("Blessed art thou, O Lord God of our fathers") and *Benedicite, omnia opera Domini* ("O all ye works of the Lord, bless ye the Lord") used in Morning Prayer.

The *Benedictus es* (vv. 29–34) carries on the psalmic tradition of tying together the idea of God as creator and lord of the universe with the idea of Zion as God's home. In it, God is blessed "in the temple of your holy glory," as the one who looks "into the depths from your throne on the cherubim," and as being "in the firmament of heaven." The *Benedicite* (vv. 35–68) continues the tradition of the wisdom psalms and calls on the whole universe to celebrate God, beginning with the angels, the heavens, the waters above the firmament, and the celestial bodies and working its way through meteorological phenomena, plants, and animals until it finally focuses on Israel.

It is uncertain whether these canticles were written originally in Greek (the oldest form in which we have them) or translated from a Hebrew or Aramaic original. The prosody is that of ancient Hebrew, but just as ancient Hebrew poetry lent itself to translation, so, too, it was relatively easy to pattern new poetry on it in other languages. We have examples of psalms that were probably composed in Greek in the Gospel of Luke, where we find poetry attributed to Mary (*Magnificat*, Luke 1:46–55), Simeon (*Nunc dimittis*, 2:29–32), and Zechariah (*Benedictus*, 1:67–79). All three of these have served throughout the ages as canticles in Christian daily prayer.

Ongoing Use of the Psalms: Psalms 24, 48, 95

The Psalter has also continued in liturgical use among both Jews and Christians. After the Roman destruction of Jerusalem in 70 CE brought the sacrificial rites of the temple to an end, the temple's songbook remained a basic expression of Jewish faith. Even before this, war, exile, and other historic forces had spread Jewish populations across much of the Near East and Mediterranean basin. Many Jews lived too far from Jerusalem to experience the Psalms in their temple setting, but the people kept on using the Psalms in the emerging context of the synagogue, which was both a community center and a place for instruction, for the reading of Torah, and for prayer.

When a written composition moves in this way from its original context into a new one, its meaning inevitably shifts somewhat. This is particularly true in worship, where the text is constantly being claimed by new voices as an expression of their own devotion under changed circumstances. Two texts we looked at earlier in our reading are good examples. **Psalm 24** (cf. Chapter 3) has an important place in Jewish daily prayers, where it no longer speaks primarily to the question of who may ascend Mt. Zion and enter into the worship of the temple. Instead, a new stress necessarily falls on its opening words:

> The *earth* is the LORD's and all that is in it,
>   the *world*, and those who live in it. . . . (24:1)

When these words were spoken in the temple, they could be heard as implying that the temple was all the more sacred. They still retain that meaning, and yet, at the same time, they verify the sanctity of every place where one may find oneself worshipping. Thus, the question "Who shall ascend the hill of the LORD?" is inevitably broadened out to interrogate the worshipper in the synagogue, too, and this worshipper will answer in the same terms:

> Those who have clean hands and pure hearts,
>   who do not lift up their souls to what is false,
>   and do not swear deceitfully. (24:4)

Psalm 48 (cf. Chapter 1) is another good example of the way distance in time and space can shift the meaning of a text. The celebration of Zion at its conclusion could no longer carry the same aura of certainty:

> Walk about Zion, go all around it,
>> count its towers,
> consider well its ramparts;
>> go through its citadels,
> that you may tell the next generation
>> that this is God,
> our God forever and ever.
>> He will be our guide forever. (48:12–14)

There must have been an edge of sadness in celebrating a city sometimes in ruins and more often than not in the hands of Gentiles. Yet, the celebration of Zion continued to define Jewish identity, not so much by devaluing the present circumstances of the worshippers, whatever they might be, but by insisting that the meaning of the present lay in its connection with both past and future, both the glory of the ancient metropolis and the hope expressed annually at Passover: next year in Jerusalem!

Christians, like Jews, are familiar with the extraordinary ability of the Psalms to express the most profound issues of faith under circumstances different from those in which they were written. In the previous chapters, we have read the Psalms primarily in terms of the time when they were written and edited. This is a valuable exercise and often illuminates language or imagery that is not fully intelligible in terms of our own day. But this kind of reading does not exhaust their meaning, which may indeed grow deeper with the intervening centuries of human experience.

Reading the Psalms primarily in terms of the time when they were written can illuminate language or imagery that is not fully intelligible in terms of our own day. But their meaning may grow deeper with the intervening centuries of human experience.

The Psalms have been essential texts for Christians from the beginning. It would be an unusual liturgy, at least among more traditional Christian churches, that did not include a psalm at some point, whether in the relatively literal style of translation that imitates Hebrew poetry or as a "metrical psalm" in the style of later Christian hymnody.

Anglicans still follow the medieval custom of reciting **Psalm 95** (known as the *Venite* from its opening word in Latin) near the beginning of the service of Morning Prayer. It functions there, to use the technical term, as an "invitatory," that is, a kind of introduction and invitation to the recitation of the other psalms that follow, varying from day to day. It offers another example of how ancient texts enter into dialogue with later circumstances.

The original choice of Psalm 95 as invitatory was probably based on its opening lines:

> O come, let us sing to the LORD;
>> let us make a joyful noise to the rock of our salvation!
> Let us come into his presence with thanksgiving;
>> let us make a joyful noise to him with songs of praise! (95:1–2)

What better choice for an invitation to prayer?

The psalm continues, in a pattern we have seen elsewhere, by celebrating God as supreme creator of all and by claiming this God as "our God" in particular and ourselves as "the people of his pasture and the sheep of his hand." And here we meet one clear shift in perspective. When the psalm was sung in the temple of Jerusalem, the "we" referred to the people of Israel worshipping there; on the lips of a Christian congregation, the "we" is a different one.

Is this in some way a misuse of the text? It can be, if Christians try to claim the Psalter as our own to the exclusion of the other heirs of ancient Israel. Hostility toward Judaism emerged early on in Christian history. Sometimes, as with the second-century teacher Marcion, it took the form of a complete rejection of the heritage from ancient Israel. At other times, it took the form of asserting that only Christians were true heirs of Israel and that Jews had got it all wrong. Either approach inevitably distorts Christian faith and does injustice to our Jewish neighbors.

When Psalm 95 was sung in the temple of Jerusalem, the "we" referred to the people of Israel worshipping there. On the lips of a Christian congregation, the "we" is a different one, but it still has to include our Jewish neighbors.

Still, our own changed context will inevitably affect the meaning of the texts we recite. We have no justification for excluding our siblings in faith from the "we" who sing to God in Psalm 95. But we do have to include ourselves:

> For he is our God,
>> and we are the people of his pasture,
>> and the sheep of his hand. (95:7)

In some sense, we even have to go beyond the specific religious traditions descended from ancient Israel and include the whole human family in this invitation. Who, after all, do we suppose is *not* one of God's sheep? And how could we think that Christians have the privilege of making such an exclusion?

Having issued this broad invitation, however, the psalm shifts direction. Indeed, God begins to speak directly to us:

> Do not harden your hearts, as at Meribah,
>> as on the day at Massah in the wilderness,
> when your ancestors tested me,
>> and put me to the proof, though they had seen my work.
>> (95:8–9)

Suddenly, we are back wandering in the wilderness (Exod 17:1–7), quarreling with this God we have claimed as our shepherd. Or, rather, we are reminded that our forebears did this and urged not to imitate them. But, wait! Were these *our* forebears, or those of our Jewish siblings? The simple answer is that, if we claim ancient Israel as our ancestors in a positive sense, we cannot exempt ourselves from identifying with the people who are being reproved in this part of the psalm. Our spiritual ancestors are not always our physical ancestors. And whether they are or not, they are likely to be both models to follow and models of what to guard against. When we join in the saying of the psalm, we acknowledge that the experience of the wilderness wandering is critical for our own spiritual journey. Indeed, we admit that we are still faced with the same kinds of decisions that our forebears faced, still challenged by the need to listen to God's voice and not harden our hearts—and still capable of failure.

We cannot include ourselves in the joyful "we" of the first verse of Psalm 95 and exempt ourselves from identifying with the people whose sin is brought to mind in its latter part. Our spiritual ancestors are likely to be both models to follow and models of what to guard against.

The psalm goes on to warn that real consequences follow on our decision. God says:

For forty years I loathed that generation
    and said, "They are a people whose hearts go astray,
    and they do not regard my ways."
Therefore in my anger I swore,
    "They shall not enter my rest." (95:10–11)

The "forty years" here refers to the story of how the period of wilderness wandering was extended to that length of time so that none of those who had been miraculously liberated from Egypt and then afterward turned against God and Moses would live to see the promised land (Num 14). Entering into God's rest is a gift, but it is a gift that we are allowed to refuse.

The summons to joyful worship, then, does not mean that we escape the challenges of life in the Spirit. We are welcome to include ourselves among God's sheep, but only if we recognize that, as God's sheep, we are still capable of betrayal and rejection. Perhaps at this point, Psalm 95 seems a bit less "inviting" than it did at first. Indeed many revisions of the Book of Common Prayer, beginning in the eighteenth century, have omitted the last four verses from the *Venite*. (This did not mean that they were never recited, since the full Psalm 95 still came up in the regular cycle.) The change could be defended on the grounds that the psalm was being used as a canticle in this case. But it is a good example of how later users of a text grapple for better or worse with its meaning in changing circumstances. We like the rejoicing part; we are not quite so happy when the psalm pulls us aside and says, "Do not compliment yourselves too much. You are still capable of wrong-doing." But we do not abandon the conversation. We keep on singing and making a joyful noise. And we also keep on asking ourselves where we may be refusing God and the rest into which God invites us. It is important for Christians to remember that we have proved capable at times of serious crimes, some of them carried out in the name of the God who warns us here of this very possibility.

The Psalms In New Testament Theology: Psalms 2, 95, 110

The use of psalms in Christian worship is rooted in the first century, when the earliest Christians retained the basic pattern of synagogue

The list of quotations from the Psalter found in the New Testament is longer than that for any other book of the Scriptures of Israel, even edging out the other overwhelming favorite, Isaiah.

worship. It is no surprise then that the Psalms crop up frequently in the earliest Christian writings. The list of New Testament quotations from and allusions to the Psalter is longer than that for any other book of the Scriptures of Israel, even edging out the other overwhelming favorite, Isaiah.

Psalm 95, for example, plays a prominent role in the Epistle to Hebrews, which uses it to make the basic point we have just been noting—that all of human life is a kind of journey through the wilderness toward the promised land, a journey that no one can take for granted. The author warns us that we are not above repeating our forebears' errors (Heb 3:7–19). At the same time, our author insists that the promised rest remains a possibility for succeeding generations and even magnifies its theological importance by associating it with God's own sabbath rest on the seventh day of creation (4:1–12).

Perhaps the single most important theological function of psalms in the New Testament, however, is to interpret the meaning of Jesus. It is hard to imagine how early Christians would have expressed and explained the importance of Christ without the help of texts such as Psalms 2 and 110. We have noted that the idea of the king survived long after the office itself disappeared, not least because it was enshrined in many of the psalms. This helped create an image of a longed-for future Anointed One, whom Christians identified with Jesus. At moments, the correspondences between certain psalms and the life of Jesus seemed so precise that Christians could think of David as a prophet who had detailed long before much of what Jesus would do and experience (e.g., Acts 1:16).

Psalms 2 and 110 both speak of the royal enthronement ceremony and provide terms that were quickly employed in the early Christians' effort to explain who they understood Jesus to be. **Psalm 2** tells us that the king was considered God's son:

> I will tell of the decree of the LORD:
> He said to me, "You are my son;
>> today I have begotten you." (2:7)

Such language was by no means rare with regard to kingly figures of antiquity. It did not mean that the king was necessarily venerated as a god. There is no sign of such an idea in ancient Israel, though it certainly existed elsewhere. People understood that the king was human and therefore mortal, even when they prayed in hyperbolic terms:

> May he live while the sun endures,
>   and as long as the moon, throughout all generations. (Ps 72:5)

Still, the king did hold immense power over the nation, a power reflecting that of God over the world. When the early Christians called Jesus "Son of God," they were drawing on this traditional royal ideology.

In Psalm 2:7, it is God who makes this proclamation of sonship. In the gospels, a divine voice addresses Jesus in these same terms at his Baptism: "And a voice came from heaven, 'You are my Son, the Beloved; with you I am well pleased.'" (Mark 1:11) Matthew's version of the story (3:17) has the voice address the crowd instead: "'This is my Son . . .'"; but the reference to the psalm is still clear. Luke 4:22, in the NRSV text, has the same phrasing as Mark; and if you consult the textual footnote, you will find that some ancient manuscripts "improved" the text to mirror the quotation from Psalm 2 more exactly: "'You are my Son, today I have begotten you.'"

> *Psalm 2 speaks of the king as God's son—language that was by no means rare in antiquity. When the early Christians called Jesus "Son of God," they were drawing on this traditional royal ideology.*

For some early Christians, it seems, this narrative meant that Jesus *became* the Son of God when the Spirit descended upon him at the Baptism. But for people like Luke, who dated the incarnation to the beginning of Jesus' life, it was, rather, a kind of coronation pronouncement, a public assertion of the Son's legitimacy. The Prologue of John's Gospel, the most explicit statement of incarnational theology in the New Testament, also has an allusion to Psalm 2:

> No one has ever seen God. It is God the only Son, who is close
> to the father's heart, who has made him known. (John 1:18)

We also have an important passage from Paul, which draws on Psalm 110 as well as Psalm 2. The passage has a poetic form, either created by Paul himself or borrowed from an existing Christian hymn about Jesus. Like the psalms, it shows parallelism in its construction:

> who, though he was in the form of God,
>> did not regard equality with God
>> as something to be exploited,
> but emptied himself,
>> taking the form of a slave,
>> being born in human likeness. (Phil 2:6–7)

The incarnate Jesus has thus shed all power, even to the point of suffering a degrading death on the cross; but, having done so, he is recognized as God's true equal, just as he was from the beginning, and given "the name that is above every name," the name of "Lord." (2:8–11).

A word of explanation is needed here. In the Hebrew Scriptures, the name of God is written but not pronounced. When people encounter it in reading the scriptures, they substitute another word, usually *adonai*, a form of *adon*, which means "lord." English translations of the Hebrew Scriptures generally make a similar substitution; but to mark where they do this, they spell the substitute word in capital letters: LORD. Thus, the English reader can tell that "LORD" represents the name of God and "Lord" or "lord" represents some other use of *adon* in the Hebrew text.

A problem arose in antiquity, however, when many Jews spoke Greek rather than Hebrew. The scholars who translated the scriptures into Greek used the Greek noun *kyrios*, "lord," to represent the name of God. And they provided an indication of this by using the noun without any definite article, which gave the expression a slightly awkward and distinctive quality. But Greek writing at the time had no absolutely clear way to distinguish when *kyrios* stood for the name of God and when for a written form of *adon*. The result was that any occurrence of *kyrios* might possibly stand for the name of God.

In Philippians, Jesus is given the name of "God" in a new sense, won not by exercising divine power but by daring to let go of this power and endure suffering and death.

What Jesus is given, then, in Philippians is the title "Lord" in the sense of the *name* of God. But doesn't the hymn say that he was in the form of God from the beginning? Yes, but now he is given the name of God in a new sense, won not by exercising divine power but by daring to let go of this power and endure suffering and death. The cross, God's greatest defeat, becomes the new source of true divine power.

The passage in Philippians draws on **Psalm 110** in a way that seems perplexing to modern readers. Ancient biblical interpreters often operated in a more associative and imaginative way than we now expect. Paul (or his source) may or may not have been proficient in Hebrew, but they felt free to develop a line of thought by building on the ambiguity in the Greek text of Psalm 110, using methods much like those the rabbis were applying to the Hebrew text. The text that lies behind our Philippians passage begins:

> The LORD says to my lord,
>> "Sit at my right hand
> until I make your enemies your footstool." (110:1)

Paul read both "lords" here as having the same meaning, so that God, "the LORD," actually addresses Jesus as "LORD." Since Paul could not distinguish the two different uses of *kyrios* in this particular passage, he was able to interpret Psalm 110 as saying something surprising about the relationship of God and Jesus. But, beyond that, he finds a message about the relation between suffering and power in the life of God as revealed in the life of Jesus. To the Jesus who has freely suffered the human lot all creatures now bend the knee, which represents their free acknowledgment of God—in contrast to the enemies' involuntary subjugation as the king's footstool in the psalm. Is this what the author of Psalm 110 had in mind? Clearly not. But it is the kind of development of themes and images that poets routinely work with, thus transforming elements of the received tradition into the raw materials for new artistic creation.

This is not the only way that Psalm 110 entered into the early Christian process of explaining who Jesus is. We are told that Jesus made use of this same passage to pose a riddle to his opponents:

> How can the scribes say that the Messiah is the son of David?
> David himself, by the Holy Spirit, declared,
>> "The Lord said to my Lord,
>> 'Sit at my right hand,
>>> until I put your enemies under your feet.'"
> David himself calls him Lord; so how can he be his son?
>> (Mark 12:35–37)

The riddle relies on the assumption that David is author of all the psalms in general and of this one in particular. Given this assumption, however, how can David address any later king as "my Lord"? Descendants can speak of their ancestors in such terms, but not the other way around. The passage thus raises a theological question about the whole idea of the Messiah. Can the Messiah be adequately understood as simply a continuation of the royal ideology of the past? No, says Jesus, some change of paradigms is necessary. The change involves, on the one hand, a vastly greater authority than that of the Davidic monarch, but also, as Paul said, a willingness to let go of power in order to descend into the human predicament.

The Letter to Hebrews uses Psalm 110 to anchor its extended theology of Jesus as eternal High Priest.

The unknown author of the Letter to Hebrews makes yet another use of Psalm 110, focusing now on its proclamation of another kind of office:

> The Lord has sworn and will not change his mind,
>> "You are a priest forever according to the order of
>> Melchizedek." (110:4)

For the ancient kings of Judah, this must have represented a claim of sacred office reaching back even before David to the pre-Israelite kings of Jerusalem. Melchizedek was king of Salem and "priest of God Most High" in the time of Abraham (Gen 14:17–20). Hebrews uses this verse of Psalm 110 as the focal text around which to evolve an extended theology of Jesus as eternal High Priest (Heb 4:14–10:25). Interestingly, this use of Psalm 110, like that of Paul in Philippians, also involves an emphasis on Jesus' voluntary sharing of the human state.

The early Christians did not approach the scriptures simply as ancient texts, but as oracles of God that would give them essential elements for deciphering the will of God in their own time. The stronger awareness of historical and cultural difference that modern people tend to carry in our intellectual toolkit may lead us to look askance at such a method. But reading the scriptures has always been a balancing act between what is old (and therefore increasingly puzzling or even unintelligible) and what is readily accessible in the text and can help readers understand the journey with God in their own time and place. Neither side of this process can be dismissed. If we try to do so, we and the text will be left isolated from each other, with no further conversation possible between us.

> *Early Christians did not approach the scriptures primarily as ancient texts, but as oracles of God that would give them essential elements for deciphering the will of God in their own time.*

This would constitute a significant diminishment of our world, which becomes spiritually and aesthetically poorer without the scriptures; it is also a contradiction of Christian experience. Again and again, Christians have found that God can and does speak to us through scripture. We find that even the most unlikely text may occasion for us new understanding of ourselves or of God, new hope, new trust, new love—all those cumulative conversions of perspective that make up our growth in the life of faith. Sometimes what we hear afresh in such a moment emerges directly from the words of the text; these are times when we indeed sense ourselves in direct conversation with people who lived thousands of years ago. But sometimes, God uses improbable connections to produce new insight. This is so, at least in part, with the theological use of the Psalms in the New Testament. Through texts like Psalms 2 and 110 the royal ideology of ancient Israel met the changed world of the first century CE and produced a new understanding of how God comes to encounter humanity and transform it.

Abandonment: Psalm 22

The theological use of the psalms we have just looked at is intellectually dense and may, for some readers, lack the very qualities that we particularly value in the Psalter—emotional directness and immediacy. The same could scarcely be said with regard to **Psalm 22**, enshrined in the Passion narrative by Jesus' quotation of it from the cross: "My God, My God, why have you forsaken me?" (Mark 15:34)

> *Psalm 22 is a supreme example of the lament genre and must always have stood out as one of the great poetic and spiritual achievements of the Psalter.*

This psalm is a supreme example of the lament genre and must always have stood out as one of the great poetic and spiritual achievements of the Psalter. It is one of the handful of psalms in which the title tells us the name of the tune to which it was sung: The Deer of the Dawn. This, in turn, suggests that its power was enhanced by the music, and we can only regret its loss.

The first part of the poem moves back and forth between portrayal of the poet's desperate state and affirmation of God's power and graciousness, but it begins in a sense of abandonment:

> My God, my God, why have you forsaken me?
>> Why are you so far from helping me, from the words of
>> my groaning?
> O my God, I cry by day, but you do not answer;
>> and by night, but find no rest. (22:1–2)

Yet, God has not ignored the needs of God's people in the past:

> Yet you are holy,
>> enthroned on the praises of Israel.
> In you our ancestors trusted;
>> they trusted, and you delivered them.
> To you they cried, and were saved;
>> in you they trusted, and were not put to shame. (22:3–5)

The psalmist is reduced to the lowest possible state: "a worm, and not human." Everyone mocks and says jeeringly:

> Commit your cause to the LORD; let him deliver—
>> let him rescue the one in whom he delights. (22:8)

Still, the psalmist testifies to having experienced God's care from the earliest time:

> On you I was cast from my birth
>> and since my mother bore me you have been my God. (22:10)

The plea "Do not be far from me" (11) leads to a set of chilling metaphors that capture the frightening sense of being under brutal attack, as if surrounded by wild bulls, by lions, by packs of dogs (12–13, 20–21). Either from fear or from some illness, the psalmist has no power to resist, indeed is close to death (14–15)—so fragile that the bones show through the flesh (17). Enemies are already planning to divide what is left (18). One last appeal to God:

But you, O LORD, do not be far away!
O my help, come quickly to my aid!
Deliver my soul from the sword,
my life from the power of the dog!
Save me from the mouth of the lion! (19–21a)

And, at last, the prayer is heard. As happens often in other laments as well, the psalm then changes direction to proclaim the fulfillment of the prayer and to make a vow. God has rescued the psalmist, who will henceforth

. . . tell of your name to my brothers and sisters;
in the midst of the congregation I will praise you . . . (22:22)

The congregation in view was, first of all, that of the temple, but the psalmist envisions it as extending even further:

All the ends of the earth shall remember
and turn to the LORD:
and all the families of the nations
shall worship before him. (22:27)

This last note spoke directly, for the earliest Christians, about their own congregations, drawn increasingly from Gentiles as well as Jews. Indeed, they found an even more explicit reference to themselves further on in the line about proclaiming God's deliverance "to a people yet unborn." (30) In the psalm itself, the phrase refers to future generations, but early Christians could also hear in it the hint of a people yet to come into existence, namely the Christian people. By the second century CE, Christian thinkers such as Tertullian would refer to the church as a *tertium genus*, a third kind of humanity alongside Jews and Gentiles.

Christians have thus read and still read this psalm as embodying the suffering of the cross—even down to the details of the story, such as the mockery of Jesus' enemies (8) and casting lots for Jesus' tunic (18). This does not, however, mean that it no longer refers to the realities of other great sufferings. It means that it acquires a new range of meanings, through its intersection with Jesus' death, without losing the old.

The Psalms in Prayer and Meditation:
Psalms 37, 84, 137, 139

Perhaps the single most important thing about the Psalms in Christian tradition is simply that they have been prayed over and over again by faithful people, taking the words of scripture as their own words. It is not always an easy matter. There is much in the Psalms that is problematic for the religious heirs of the psalmists, whether Jewish or Christian. I once knew a rabbinic student who, in reciting **Psalm 37**, always fell silent for one particular verse:

> I have been young, and now am old,
>> yet I have not seen the righteous forsaken
>> or their children begging bread. (37:25)

Perhaps the single most important thing about the Psalms in Christian tradition is simply that they have been prayed over and over again by faithful people, taking the words of scripture as their own words. It is not always an easy matter.

When I asked him about this practice, he said simply that he was still young and had already seen the righteous forsaken and could not honestly repeat such a claim.

He did not therefore reject the rest of the psalm, though it taught much the same lesson—which was, for that matter, a standard part of the stock of ancient wisdom. Its aim was to reassure faithful people who are suffering persecution that truth and justice will eventually win out:

> Do not fret because of the wicked;
>> do not be envious of wrongdoers,
> for they will soon fade like the grass,
>> and wither like the green herb.
> Trust in the LORD, and do good;
>> so you will live in the land, and enjoy security.
> Take delight in the LORD,
>> and he will give you the desires of your heart. (37:1–4)

Many people going through difficult times have found some comfort in this wisdom. People in power do sometimes appear to be untouchable, free to manipulate justice for their own ends and immune to retribution. Sometimes the evil may indeed die rich and apparently happy. But this is not, says the psalmist, inevitable. The mistake is for the righteous to imagine that the power of the wicked can keep them safe. No matter how difficult the life of faithful people becomes,

> Better is a little that the righteous person has
>   than the abundance of many wicked. (37:16)

The rabbinic student was willing to join in the hope that the psalm holds out, but, at the same time, he did not compromise the integrity of his own experience. This is exactly the kind of ongoing conversation between ancient text and subsequent reader that has always characterized the prayerful, meditative use of the Psalter. The Psalter has been a school of prayer to generations of faithful people—not only clergy and vowed religious (monks and nuns), whose vocation involves repeated recitation and study of the Psalms, but also lay people who may have less time for prayer but have found the psalms a powerful expression of their relationship with God.

One thing in particular we learn from the Psalms—frankness in our conversation with God. The feelings and ideas expressed in the Psalms are not always ones we can endorse. But the honesty of their expression is something we ought to imitate. After all, if we conceal who we are and what we feel or think when we pray, we are not fully engaged with God; we are trying, in effect, to protect that part of us that may most need to be revealed and submitted to the possibility of transformation. It is better to pray in ways that reveal what is unlovely about us than to try to cover the truth up and thereby wind up not fully present in our own prayer.

The most extreme example of this is probably the conclusion of **Psalm 137**, which has caused untold trouble to generations of faithful readers and meditators. The psalm opens with a powerful image of the misery of exile:

> By the rivers of Babylon—
>   there we sat down and there we wept
>   when we remembered Zion.
> On the willows there
>   we hung up our harps.

For there our captors
    asked us for songs,
and our tormentors asked for mirth, saying,
    "Sing us one of the songs of Zion!" (137:1–3)

There follows an anguished vow to remember lost Jerusalem and set it "above my highest joy." The psalm was surely written early in the Exile, when the pain of loss was at its deepest. We are not surprised, having read other laments, to find that a curse on enemies follows— first against the Edomites, neighbors of Judah who sided with the Babylonians, then against Babylon itself. But we are not prepared for the last verse to turn this curse into a horrible blessing on the killing of children.

> Better to blurt out even our worst hatreds and let them stand in the light of God's generous will. Only that daring kind of prayer can begin the process of conversion.

The overall context of scripture, whether the Scriptures of Israel or the Christian Bible, tells the faithful clearly that this is not a permissible form of vengeance. Would it be better if this verse were erased from the psalm? I think probably not. Better to blurt out even our hatreds and let them stand in the light of God's generous will. Only in this daring kind of prayer can we begin the process of conversion from anguish and anger, however justified by our oppression, to the hopeful perspective of a God who is looking for ways to build a future of peace in the creation.

Psalm 137 is unique in this particular expression of brutal retaliation, but not in the way in which our most generous and our most hostile capacities can stand alongside each other. **Psalm 139** is, as a whole, one of the supreme expressions of trust in the Psalter. It begins with a moving account of authentic experience with God:

O LORD, you have searched me out and known me.
You know when I sit down and when I rise up;
    you discern my thoughts from far away. (139:1–2)

To be so completely known may not be an entirely comforting thing. Indeed, the psalmist at least toys with the idea of trying to escape it:

Where can I go from your spirit?
　Or where can I flee from your presence?
If I ascend to heaven, you are there;
　if I make my bed in Sheol, you are there. (139:7–8)

Yet, it remains clear that God's presence is motivated by love of the most expansive sort:

For it was you who formed my inward parts;
　you knit me together in my mother's womb.
I praise you, for I am fearfully and wonderfully made.
　Wonderful are your works;
that I know very well.
　My frame was not hidden from you,
when I was being made in secret,
　intricately woven in the depths of the earth. (139:13–15)

"The depths of the earth" serves as a parallel to the mother's womb, but, at the same time, the phrase expands the particularity of one mother's womb to associate it with the whole creative process which has led to human life. Our birth is from both a mother and from the whole life of creation.

The psalmist is daunted by the vastness of this whole vision—and at the same time wholly caught up in it:

How weighty to me are your thoughts, O God!
　How vast is the sum of them!
I try to count them—they are more than the sand;
　I come to the end—I am still with you. (139:17–18)

It is startling, then, to find that the poet emerges from this meditation with curses:

O that you would kill the wicked, O God,
　and that the bloodthirsty would depart from me. . . .
Do I not hate those who hate you, O LORD?
. . . .
I hate them with perfect hatred. . . . (139:19–22)

Eventually, we recognize that we may be, in ways we do not yet understand, part of the enemy we hate. Only God can enable us to grow in discernment and to follow "the way everlasting."

But then, in another reversal, the psalm begs God to examine our own hearts and lead us in the right way. The telling thing in such a meditation is that the truly humble will not be able, in the end, to exempt themselves from the curse on sinners. Only the arrogant will imagine that they can feel completely secure in their curses. What pulls us back from even our most intensely felt hatreds is the recognition that we may be, in ways we do not yet understand, part of what we hate. Others, indeed, may find reason to direct their curses at us. Only God can enable us to grow in discernment and to follow "the way everlasting."

This kind of prayerful and meditative reading is by no means some later imposition on the Psalter. The editors of the text invited it by placing, at its head, **Psalm 1**, with its blessing on those whose

> delight is in the law of the LORD,
>   and on his law they meditate day and night. (1:2)

Their inclusion of Psalm 119—an ungainly component in a collection made up mostly of much shorter pieces—also emphasizes the virtue of meditation. Of course, any part of scripture may serve as a focus of meditation, but the Psalms actually launch the process with us by their insistence on speaking almost entirely in the voice not of prophecy nor law nor narrative but of the actual worshipper. They say to their readers of every age, "Come, join in this age-long approach to God in worship, exposing yourself to judgment and to love, turning the deep complexity and the profound simplicity of our relationship with God over and over in your mind and heart and opening yourself to new understanding."

Psalm 84 gives us the hymn "How lovely is thy dwelling place" and also the text to perhaps the best-loved section of Brahms's German Requiem.

Perhaps my choice of psalms here has left the impression that this is always a difficult and often a painful process. That would be an unfair impression to leave with my readers. The difficulties are there—and have to be there because they reflect our own personal divisions and failures as well as the challenges of human life in the times of the psalmists. But the joys are there, too. **Psalm 84** speaks to us as directly as the much loved Psalm 23, drawing us into God's presence through the image of the temple where the Psalms once found themselves at home:

> How lovely is your dwelling place,
>   O Lord of hosts!
> My soul longs, indeed it faints
>   for the courts of the Lord;
> my heart and my flesh sing for joy
>   to the living God. (84:1–2)

There follows a verbal picture of the temple's open courts, with birds nesting on roofs and walls, with choirs of singers, and with approaching pilgrims (some of whom will have come through the Valley of Baca or "weeping"). All this gives substance to the longed-for goal:

> For a day in your courts is better
> than a thousand elsewhere.
> I would rather be a doorkeeper in the house of my God
> than live in the tents of wickedness. (84:10)

To sum up not only this psalm, but in some sense the entire hope of scripture:

> O Lord of hosts,
>   happy is everyone who trusts in you. (84:12)

At any given moment of our lives, we shall have our favorites among the Psalms—and those that seem to have nothing to say to us or even repel us. One of the virtues of reading and re-reading them, of repeated meditation on them, is that, collectively, they provide us with a language of thought and prayer for every season of life—even those we cannot now imagine. And—first, last, and always—they inculcate a practice of complete openness with God that is the only healthy context for growth in the life of faith.

The Never-Ending Song

We began this study of the book of Psalms by emphasizing the link between these poems and the temple in Jerusalem. Yet, it was never possible—and probably never intended—to limit their use. Many of the psalms must have gone to Babylonia with the exiles of Judah and Jerusalem. They played a role in the emergence of synagogue worship there, a kind of worship that would sustain Jewish people for millennia to come. And even though the sacrificial worship that had anciently formed the focal point of Israel's relationship with God could be practiced nowhere but in Jerusalem, the Psalms helped to connect the worship of the synagogue with the altar of sacrifice there—even after the Second Temple, too, had been destroyed.

Christians, like Jews, made ongoing use of the Psalms in their worship, so that we, too, are linked by them with the holy place of Zion, which has filled the Christian imagination in ways that still characterize and shape our language of prayer. The Psalms have pervaded Christian worship in many languages and a wide range of musical forms. Like Jews, Christians at first left behind the musical instruments and the loud dynamics of the temple's music. Church music, for a long time (and still in the Christian East) was purely vocal. But we sang about praising God with trumpets, lutes, harps, tambourines, strings, pipes, cymbals—all the musical panoply of Psalm 150. And in the Christian West of the Middle Ages, the instruments began to make their return and the Psalms regained some of their former loud splendor, albeit in musical modes dramatically different from those of Israelite antiquity.

The last reference to the temple in the Christian scriptures occurs in the Revelation of John—and it negates the temple in order to make it universal: "I saw no temple in the city, for its temple is the Lord God the Almighty and the Lamb." (21:22) The Heavenly Jerusalem, according to John, has no need of a temple, a place of sacrifice, because God, in the Age to Come, will live on a footing of perfect intimacy with God's people. This does not, however, mean the end of music. Revelation is full of music. The throne of God reverberates with "rumblings and peals of thunder" (4:5). The four living creatures around the throne sing "day and night without ceasing"

(4:8), joined by the twenty-four elders with voice and harp (5:8). The volume of sound is immense "like the sound of many waters and like the sound of loud thunder" (14:2). The songs, then, will outlive the earthly temple and, in this age and in the Age to Come, still have the power they have always had.

Continuing the Conversation:

Those interested in the psalmic literature of Qumran will find it in the English translations of the Dead Sea Scrolls by Geza Vermes and by Florentino García Martínez (originally in Spanish).

One example of the Christian tradition of meditating on the Psalms is Barbara Green, *Like a Tree Planted: An Exploration of Psalms and Parables Through Metaphor* (Collegeville: Liturgical Press, 1997).

STUDY QUESTIONS

Sharon Ely Pearson

The book of Psalms is often referred to as "the Psalter," both words coming from a Greek word designating a stringed instrument. Many have compared the Psalter to the hymnals used in Christian churches for worship services, including our world today. One can learn a great deal about the varying outlooks on faith of a people by reading the hymns they sing. What can the Psalms teach us about the richness of human life—the joy, despair, anger, doubt and faith—that worship life of Judaism in the post-exilic period reveal? Can these hymns speak to us today?

Introduction

This study guide is meant to accompany each chapter as a means to go deeper and reflect upon the Psalms as the author unpacks the various types of Psalms. The questions and reflections will invite you into a conversation about how the Psalms and themes discussed may still offer guidance to how God is leading us in the way we ought to (and need to) go in today's world. The "paths of righteousness" as translated by Dr. Countryman as "the way that contributes to the well-being of our lives and of the world around us, the way that will bring us home" offer us a vision as to how the Psalms may speak to us today.

The book of Psalms in its present form is the product of post-exilic Judaism. As it reflects the liturgical practice of this period, we can speak of it as the "Hymnbook of the Second Temple." Although it is suggested that the psalms were sung in public worship, we cannot be sure of the details. This collection of 150 songs of praise, prayers, and spiritual poems may have served as the hymnbook or prayer book of the First Temple (952–587 BCE) or Second Temple (515 BCE–70 CE), as well as the synagogues that first emerged in the Persian era. The Psalms are difficult to date. The safest conclusion is that they originated in various periods and had a long and varied history of use. The collection in its present form shows signs of having been shaped in response to the crisis of the Exile and its aftermath. Above all, the Psalms are suited for teaching us about God, humankind, and the life of faith.

As you begin this study of the Psalms, consider the following:

- Why you are engaging in this study of the Psalms?
- What have your previous understandings and opinions of the Psalter been? Do you go into this study with any preconceived notions? If so, jot them down before reading.
- What do you hope to learn and discern for yourself in this study?
- Select your favorite psalms and memorize them or at least the portions you find most important. How do they affect your prayer life?
- As you read a variety of psalms along with Dr. Countryman's commentary, list situations in your own life to which the psalm may apply. List the areas of possible application to the church communities in which you are involved. Choose one item from these two lists to think about. As you go about your daily life such as going for an appointment, commuting, sitting at your desk, going for a walk, wonder about the passage as it applies to your situation. Bring the Psalms to your time of daily prayer.

Before each chapter section of this study guide, portions of scripture will be suggested to read ahead of time. If possible, choose several translations of the Bible, including the NRSV and King James Version, as well as The Hymnal 1982 and 1979 Book of Common Prayer. Many of the psalms are found in our hymnal; your study group may enjoy singing one of them to begin or conclude each of your sessions.

At the end of each chapter, additional resources are also suggested for continuing the conversation in your study group or on your own.

Introduction: I Know "The LORD Is My Shepherd":
Why Would I Want to Study the Psalms?

This introduction sets the scene for our study of the Psalms.

Read Psalm 23 in the NRSV as well as the KJV.
- What does the image of a shepherd conjure up for you?
- What way is God leading you?
- Why do you read scripture?
- How are the Psalms different from other books of the Bible?

Chapter One—"Praise God in His Sanctuary . . .":
Songs for the Temple

Read the following Psalms before reading the beginning of Chapter One:
- Psalm 150
- Psalm 135
- Psalm 149
- Psalm 135
- Psalm 29
- Psalm 68
- Psalm 82
- Psalm 47
- Psalm 87
- Psalm 26
- Psalm 27
- Psalm 48

First, we take a look at what some of the psalms tell us about the temple and its worship, particularly the part that music and song played in it.
- Why did the temple have such an important role in the religion of ancient Israel?
- Do our sanctuaries hold the same place in our faith tradition?
- What is your understanding of where God's presence is?
- What is the purpose of music in worship?
- What metaphors in nature do you have to represent God, if any?
- What is necessary for you to praise God? For a church? For a nation?
- How did God shift from being one among many gods to being the only God? Is this relevant to our world today? How?
- Is the statement, "God is, in the fundamental sense, God even of those who do not yet know it" true today?
- How is reading the Psalms like reading the history of Israel?

Reflect upon Dr. Countryman's statement, "The Psalter is, after all, framed as expressing human thoughts, not, on the whole, those of God. This will inevitably include some thoughts that we normally censor. In fact, the Psalms stand in sharp contrast to our frequent presupposition that prayer should present only our best face to God. That more polite model of prayer may not always incorporate our full humanity or push us toward such deep self-examination" (p. 16).

Assembling the Psalter: Read Psalm 137, 1 Samuel 16:14–23, Psalms 14, 53, and 114.
- Why are the psalms attributed to David?
- What hymns do we have in The Hymnal 1982 that include "Hallelujah" or "Alleluia"? How are they similar (or different) to the "hallels"?
- What names do you use for God?
- How have you read the Psalms in the past?

Chapter Two "You That Stand in the House of the LORD": The World of the Psalmists

Chapter Two begins with a discussion of language and culture. Do you agree or disagree with the following statements? Why or why not?
- Every language has its limitations and its blind spots.
- The Psalms have become sacred classics of world literature.
- Cultural change happens even in the most stable societies, which means that we may observe some elements of change within this distant culture. What are the elements of change that you observe?
- Men are the audience of these poems; it is a cultural assumption about gender roles. How is this different (or the same) today in literature, worship, hymns, prayer, and our society?

Read Psalms 120–134 as you deepen your reading of Chapter Two regarding pilgrimages to the temple.
- What people live in a diaspora today? How might the Psalms resonate with them?
- How would "Peace be within you" be a prayer for prosperity, justice, and well-being that benefits all alike? How might we use this in conversation or prayer today?
- How would you characterize the Psalms of Ascent for you/us today?

- How do we "translate" the cultural presuppositions of the Psalms into our own changed circumstances?

The Moral Agent, the King, Marriage, Justice, Peace, and the Community: Read Psalms 1, 89, 45, 93, 72, and 115.

- Why do you believe it is such a challenge to translate the Psalms to today's audience?
- What are the similarities between a king and a priest? Differences? Where do the two continue to merge in the world today? Why was it needed to combine both roles in the Jewish community?
- What is the meaning of kingship to you? How is this expressed in the Psalms?
- What were the instruments of royal power? Which psalms resonate with you in connecting with your belief of what kingship is?
- How has marriage continued to connect royalty within a nation or to cement foreign alliances today? How is this similar to political alliances in a democratic society?
- What's the difference between creation and conquest as described in the Psalms? Similarities?
- Why was a king as a just judge central to Israel?
- Compare Psalm 72 with James Montgomery's hymn "Hail to the Lord's Anointed" (The Hymnal 1982 #616).
- Why is there always a desire to guard the traditions of worship?
- How did the collision of empires make possible a century of Jewish independence where priests and kings held the same role until the coming of the Roman Empire?

Chapter Three—"O Sing to the LORD a New Song": Hymns of Praise and Songs of Worship

Many of the psalms are categorized as hymns of praise to God. The praise may be for God's general work of creation, for God's care and protection to an individual or to Israel itself, for thanksgiving when God has delivered the people from affliction, or for all the wonderful things that God has done during the history of Israel.

Poetry: Read Psalm 23 again.
- Following the method of how Countryman describes this familiar psalm, construct your own psalm depicting God or praising God.
- How is ancient poetry similar (or different) to the poetry of the modern world?

Hymns: Read Psalms 97, 98, 99, 100, 103, 105, and 117.
- Choose one of your favorite praise hymns from The Hymnal 1982. How is it like a summons to praise God followed by a list of reasons?
- Why do the Psalms retain the theme of the reign of God, made tangible in God's day of judgment, vindicating the whole world? Why does this thread weave its way throughout the Psalter?
- What motifs does Countryman offer that are repeated in the Psalms? Would you add others?

Style and Liturgy: Read Psalms 46, 107, and 136 and Psalms 24, 121, 132, and 104.
- Compare Martin Luther's hymn "A mighty fortress is our God" (The Hymnal 1982 #688) with Psalm 46. How are they similar?
- How does Psalm 107 point toward the hope of a continuing restoration of Israel through return from exile? With whom might this psalm resonate in today's world?
- How does are the psalms read each Sunday in your congregation? Are they sung by the congregation, choir, or cantor? Read by one person or as a call-and-response? How does this enhance or detract from your appreciation and understanding of the appointed psalms/s of the day?
- How do hymns embrace a diverse array of the perspectives on God from your viewpoint?
- How is liturgy like a pilgrimage to visit God in God's holy temple?
- Countryman states that a hymn consists of two elements, a summons to praise and a reason for praising. Does this hold true for the popular hymns of today?

■ How does Psalm 104 serve as an example of creation, sin, judgment, and redemption?

Chapter Four—"I Am Weary with My Crying": Psalms of Lament, Trust, and Thanksgiving

In laments, the cry of the afflicted is raised to God, asking for relief. Some of the laments appear to have been composed by individuals facing personal difficulties; others speak of the suffering of a nation. Their language and imagery suggest sickness, persecution by false accusers, and warfare. Whether individual or communal, the laments provide ways for the worshiping community to bring its cry to God.

Laments: Read Psalms 69, 9, 80, 90, 28, and 41.
■ Following the method of how Countryman describes this genre of psalm, construct your own psalm expressing distress over suffering or loss while asking for God's intervention. Use these elements: address to God; statement of problem; request for help; affirmation of trust; and a vow to be fulfilled.
■ Why does this psalm make a shift from the needs and desires from an individual to that of the community?
■ What is the difference between "I" and "we" when we pray?
■ Which of the lament psalms speaks most to you? What was the circumstance you associated with it?
■ Find Hymn #680 ("O God, our help in ages past") by Isaac Watts in The Hymnal 1982. How does this compare to Psalm 90?
■ How would you characterize the difference between individual and community laments?

Confession: Read Psalms 50, 51 and 2 Samuel 12:1–31.
■ How does the psalmist wrestle with God?
■ How does David wrestle with God?
■ Why is forgiveness often framed in the language of purification? Where is this also captured in our sacramental liturgies and language?
■ What is the purpose of sacrifice?
■ How would you describe the holy spirit of God in the Psalms (as opposed to our Christian understanding of the Holy Spirit)?

Trust and Thanksgivings: Read Psalms 130, 131 and 18, 30, 118.
- Compare the psalms of lament with these two psalms associated with trust.
- How is a song of trust like a love poem to God?
- How may the Psalms serve as models for prayers of thanksgiving?
- How does the non-existence of an afterlife make these psalms more powerful?
- Find Hymn #658 ("As longs the deer for cooling streams") and compare it with Psalms 41 and 42. How do these resonate with you as an example of a lament with its components of sadness, retaliation, restoration, and hope?

Chapter Five—"The Heavens Are Telling the Glory of God": Psalms of Wisdom

Wisdom psalms are neither songs of praise nor prayers. They are spiritual poems that offer reflections or advice concerning the faithful life or the Torah. "Wisdom" in ancient Israel reflected on the whole range of human experience—from good table manners to theodicy (resolving evil via God's justice and benevolence), from nature to ethics. Wisdom draws all of human experience into the contemplation of God's work.

Read Psalm 19.
- Compare Hymn #409, Joseph Addison's "The spacious firmament on high," with Psalm 19.
- Where do you hear the ethical dimensions of human life?
- How does the psalmist move from creation through to redemption in his writings?
- How is faith in God intersecting with daily human experience in Psalm 19?

Celebrating the Creator: Read Psalms 65 and 104.
- What type of psalm would you write to express your concern for creation?
- Search for other psalms that have an environmental theme, that of caring or celebrating creation.

- Why does wisdom seem so connected to nature and environmental action?

Reflecting on Humanity: Read Psalms 8, 33, and 146.
- How is humankind reflected in these psalms?
- What is the relationship between God and humanity?

The Law of God: Read Psalms 78 and 119.
- How are stories revealed in the Psalms?
- What is the theological function of violence and vengeance in the Psalms?
- How can psalms be used to teach history?
- Why does Torah play an important role in the Psalms?
- One of the striking things about some psalms is the theme that the study of Torah makes one wise and happy ("blessed"). How is happiness portrayed in the Psalms, and how does this differ from the varied definitions of happiness today?

The Human Community and Questioning God: Read Psalms 14, 15, and 53 and 39, 49 and 73.
- What is foolishness?
- Of what significance is it that "the righteous" in the Psalms are those who constantly find themselves to be the afflicted, poor, persecuted, and needy?
- What is your understanding of Countryman's statement, "The real issue of atheism, for the poet, is less a matter of belief than of behavior. In fact, belief here is deduced from behavior" (p. 103)?
- How is being "let alone" by God an act of extreme humility as found in Psalm 39?
- Does God's intimate presence and friendship gained in worship give you a sense of security?

The Ethos of Justice: Read Psalm 101 and 67.
- What is justice?
- What is civic integrity?
- What is the duty of government?

- Where else in scripture do we hear an insistence on righteousness and justice as matter of creating a just and livable social order with concern for the poor and the least?
- What is the theological function of violence and vengeance in the Psalms?

Chapter Six—"One Generation Shall Laud Your Works to Another": The Ongoing Influence of the Psalms

In the concluding chapter, Countryman adds additional pieces of Hebrew Scriptures and the Christian Testament, noting that they are psalm-like poems. Read one or more of the following, many of which can also be found in the 1979 Book of Common Prayer (BCP). How are these similar to other psalms that have been discussed? What genre would you categorize them?

- The Song of Moses and Miriam—Exodus 15:1–21 and BCP p. 85
- The Thanksgiving of Hannah—1 Samuel 2:1–10
- The Song of David—2 Samuel 22:1–51
- The Prayer of Sirach—Sirach 51:1–12
- The Song of the Three Jews (Young Men)—Canticle 12, BCP p. 47 or 88 and Canticle 13, BCP p. 49 or 90
- Song of Mary (*Magnificat*)—Luke 1:46–55 or BCP p. 50 or 91
- Song of Simeon (*Nunc dimittis*)—Luke 2:29–32 or BCP p. 51 or 93
- Song of Zechariah (*Benedictus*)—Zechariah 1:67–79 or BCP p. 50 or 92

Ongoing Use of the Psalms: Read Psalms 24, 48, 95.

- How does the text change through history (time and space) in our worship? What causes this?
- How are the Psalms used today as essential texts for a Christian context?
- Review how the various psalms are incorporated in Morning Prayer Rite I (BCP p. 37–53) or Rite II (BCP p. 75–96) and Evening Prayer Rite I (BCP p. 61–66) or Rite II (BCP p. 115–120).
- When we pray, to whom do you refer to when "we" appears in the psalm or prayer?

- What are your thoughts about Countryman's statement, "Who, after all, do we suppose is *not* one of God's sheep? And how could we think that Christians have the privilege of making such an exclusion?" (p. 114)?
- How are we faced with the same experiences of pilgrimage and journey as those who first experience the Psalms?

The Psalms in the New Testament: Read Psalms 2, 95, and 110 as well as John 1:14–18, Philippians 2:6–11, and Hebrews 3:7—5:10. Finally, read Psalm 22.

- How and why did the first Christians interpret the Psalms?
- How could the Psalms lead to statements of incarnational theology—Jesus as the Son of God?
- How do the psalms noted above correspond to the selections from John, Philippians, and Hebrews in the New Testament?
- How are reading the scriptures a balancing act between what is old and what is readily available in the text we read with our own eye and in our own time and space?
- How does God speak to you through scripture?
- Psalm 22 may be just as familiar to us as Psalm 23, but for very different reasons. How does this psalm follow the pattern of lament as discussed in Chapter Four? How has this become part of the Passion narrative we hear each Holy Week in our liturgies?

The Psalms in Prayer and Mediation: Read Psalms 37, 84, 137, and 139.

- How may the Psalms serve as models for prayer?
- What psalms have you found comforting in your life, if any?
- How is Psalm 137 an example of "talking frankly with God"?
- Have you ever been brutally honest with God? What does it take (and take out of you) to articulate your thoughts and feelings?
- How can the Psalms help us grow in discernment and follow "the way everlasting"?
- Compare Hymn #517 ("How lovely is thy dwelling place") with Psalm 84.

Concluding Thoughts:

- What are the most significant insights you have gleaned from reading the Psalms? Where have you been surprised and where have you been challenged?
- How may the Psalms serve as a model for your continuing prayer?
- Which psalms have resonated with you the most? Why?
- How different are you for having engaged in this study?
- What is God calling you to do in light of your study?

Sharon Ely Pearson is the Christian Formation Specialist for Church Publishing Incorporated / Morehouse Education Resources. She lives in Norwalk, Connecticut.

A PERSONAL
INTRODUCTION

When the committee responsible for Conversations with Scripture first asked me to write this volume, I protested that they had the wrong person. Yes, I am a scholar of scripture and have read Psalms both in Hebrew and (more regularly) in the ancient Greek translation. But my specialty is early Christian literature, not the Scriptures of Israel. When they proved persistent, I began to think that their interest must have something to do with the fact that I have written a good deal in the field of Christian spirituality, for which the Psalms have long been central. That, and perhaps the fact that I am a poet and my book *Lovesongs and Reproaches* bears obvious marks of the psalmists' influence.

Their persistence—along with the encouragement of my sister Betty Keely and many years of hearing fellow worshippers at Good Shepherd Episcopal Church in Berkeley saying "What was *that* about?" after the reading of the psalm—eventually prompted me to go ahead with the work. As a result, this book is less focused on the current state of Psalms scholarship (though I have tried to write in awareness of it) than it is on the poetic and spiritual values of the Psalms and on their reception into Christian worship.

I am Emeritus Professor of Biblical Studies at the Church Divinity School of the Pacific, the Episcopal Church's seminary in Berkeley, California. I also taught in the doctoral program at the Graduate Theological Union there. Before coming to California, I was a parish priest and a professor in several parts of the United States: Oklahoma, where I was born and raised; Ohio; Illinois; Missouri; and

Texas. Since retiring in 2007, I have continued to write, preach, and teach, but I am grateful also to have more time for the garden.

My spouse, Jon Vieira, and I live in Oakland, California, a big, complex, challenging, and wonderful city across the Bay from San Francisco. We rejoice in the friends that we have found here over many years, and, though we are not "native sons" of California, we are deeply rooted in this remarkable place.